Sometimes
a Woman Needs
a Horse

Sometimes a Woman Needs a Horse

A Personal Story of Discovery
of a Spiritual Message in the Horse and Rider Experience

Betsy Talcott Kelleher

Pleasant Word

Packaged by Pleasant Word, PO Box 428, Enumclaw, WA 98022. The views expressed or implied in this work do not necessarily reflect those of Pleasant Word. The author(s) is ultimately responsible for the design, content and editorial accuracy of this work.

Unless otherwise noted, all Scriptures are taken from the Holy Bible, New International Version, Copyright © 1973, 1978, 1984 by the International Bible Society. Used by permission of Zondervan Publishing House. The "NIV" and "New International Version" trademarks are registered in the United States Patent and Trademark Office by International Bible Society.

Scripture references marked PHILLIPS are taken from J. B. Phillips: The New Testament in Modern English, Revised Edition. © J. B. Phillips 1958, 1960, 1972. Used by permission of Macmillan Publishing Company.

ISBN 1-4141-0261-5
Library of Congress Catalog Card Number: 2004096031

Photo Credits

Cover Photo by Brent Hanson

Cover Photo subject: Kathy Young as a teen-ager, now a trainer and riding instructor in Florida, with Honey Pot, a thoroughbred. Kathy is the daughter of Mel and Connie Owens.

Back cover photo of Betsy with her Quarter horse gelding, Traveller, by Russ Kelleher.

Several photos of horses, people, and events mentioned in this book have been placed in a section titled "Betsy's Photo Album" at the end of the book.

"Enjoy the journey and the memories with me!"

I dedicate this book . . .

IN MEMORY of my grandfather, Lyman E. Moats, who told me countless horse stories and said he'd get me a horse someday when he found the right one . . .

AND TO ALL THE PEOPLE God brought into my life who have had a special part in my experiences of personal growth and learning about horses . . .

To my family, who did not understand my horsey world, but helped clean stalls, fixed fences, fed horses when I was away, and listened to endless talk about horses . . .

To Pam . . . who does understand and has given so very much . . .

To Linda, Judy, Connie, and Cynthia, instructors and friends, and to Stella who has gone on before us . . .

To Sally Swift, a very special lady and riding instructor . . .

To a young woman whose name is forgotten, who once said to me, "I think God puts these things in our hearts for a reason . . ."

To another young woman whose name is unknown, who rode her gray Arabian in the Coliseum when I happened to be watching, and who unknowingly became my special inspiration . . .

To Russ . . . who came into my life with the kind of love I'd always wanted . . .

And to many, many others who encouraged, listened or shared with me in a special way, and to Bob and Will who helped with the final task . . .

I give you all my deepest thanks. For anyone who has ever known that special bond with a horse . . . I share this true story, hoping that you might also find a precious relationship with the horse's Creator. I thank God for the insights He has shown me and I pray that I have passed them on with my best efforts, accurately, and compassionately.

Betsy Talcott Kelleher

Table of Contents

Introduction

*F*anny came into my life when I most needed a horse. Furthermore, Fanny was exactly the right horse . . . not just any horse could have done what she did for me. *And only God could have worked out the details the way they happened.*

Sometimes, a woman needs a horse to help her find her true self. When two separate beings learn to work together within a special bond, it becomes a partnership that strengthens both beings. Fanny was strong minded and full of spirit and energy; the kind of horse that always wanted to be boss . . . but she tried to do whatever I asked of her. She gave herself and all that she was to me with loyalty and a gentle affection, even as she remained true to her own personality. I think I *needed* her strength and energy even while that same strength and energy was at first very intimidating!

I had wanted a horse all my life . . . as much as I wanted a home of my own. I'd had a good home as a child, with a good dad and wonderful grandparents . . . but a mom was missing. I wanted a home of my own so much that I may have rushed into marriage too soon. Like most brides, I dreamed of having my own china, my own silverware pattern and delicate stemware on a table set with flowers . . . a home decorated with my own taste, color, and style.

My marriage didn't work out the way I thought it would. *I was still lonely.* I was hungry for the "oneness" I expected from a marriage. In spite of counseling, reading countless books, and my endless begging, my husband kept telling me to be satisfied with what I had. For forty-two years, I held on, hoping God would fix my marriage and it would become the partnership I felt I needed!

Seven years after our marriage, I found myself searching for more in a spiritual direction. God led me to find a new beginning of hope and peace in a close relationship with His Son Jesus! Even though I'd grown up in a Christian family, I learned I had to make my own decision about God's place in my life. If I wanted more, I would have to give more of myself to Him. *Unfortunately, I struggled with a deep fear of "total" commitment.*

Seven years later, when we bought our first country home, God led me to a horse. When Fanny came along, I didn't like her at first . . . I wanted her mother, Honey. But it seemed that God had a plan of His own and He gave only Fanny. And when I chose a trainer for her, He put one obstacle after another in my path . . . until I asked Him what I should do . . . and Pam appeared on the scene. She helped me develop the special partnership with Fanny that taught me much about connection and submission.

I believe that God had His own plan all along regarding my experiences with Fanny. *As I trained her with Pam's guidance, God appeared to be training me.* I found insight I might never have found any other way. And when Fanny's time on earth was up, the circumstances of her death and burial seemed orchestrated by a Higher Power. Looking back on my time with Fanny, I wish I had done more with her while I had her. Perhaps we all feel that way about our lives at one time or another.

Fanny was always strong willed, just like me . . . always tense, trying to figure things out instead of just listening, again like me, but I loved her. Thirteen years after losing her, I still ride her often in my dreams. As much as I loved Fanny in spite of her contrary nature, I know that God's love for me as I am is even greater. I am also aware that Fanny and I could have accomplished so much more together if I'd been more disciplined . . . just as I know my own submission to God's will could accomplish more in my own life.

This book is a small slice of autobiography, though my desired theme is to present the "horse and rider experience" as a model of God at work in human lives. I wish my readers to see God's hand in my experiences with Fanny, and to understand just how His love, wisdom, and power can guide a human life—much like a rider influences his horse. The key to it all is the submission of one being to another in response to being loved. As the submission of a horse to its rider in willing partnership can produce a brilliant performance, just so can the submission of our wills to God's sovereign guidance bring about a glorious and eternal purpose far beyond our human understanding and ability.

The greatest part of the story is that every morning is a new beginning and God's power can help me as much as I allow Him to work in and through me. I have the potential to do more to-day than I've ever done before. *And the insights I gained from my experiences with Fanny are still available as I continue to relearn them and to apply them to the present.*

A year before losing Fanny, I met a man who became my best friend. In spite of my conviction against divorce, I finally chose to stop living in misery and loneliness to pursue the relationship of "oneness" I'd always wanted with a husband. At one point, this man had a good horse that he almost sold because he couldn't "bond" with it. When he reached for the horse, the horse turned away and he didn't know how to "fix" that. I had a similar experience with my first marriage. On a human level, when you say, "I love you," you want someone to say, "I love you" back. For some rea-son that horse couldn't. And my first husband couldn't, even after forty-two years! But Russ could. And I needed so much to hear it! Relation-ships help to shape our lives in positive or nega-tive ways . . . and our relationships can become our most precious learning experiences!

Most of this book was written during the years while Fanny was still alive. A few chapters have been added or revised since her death. I have another horse now, a wonderful gelding with good manners and personality, one that is very willing and submissive . . . but sometimes I wish he was a little more like Fanny. As always, my horse's energy gives me joy . . . and Traveller does not have the same energetic drive as Fanny did. As I grow older, I appreciate a quieter horse.

But I will always remember Fanny.

"Fanny"
May 5, 1970–January 28, 1991

CHAPTER 1

"Dompa's Girl"

When I was twenty, I thought my greatest need was for a husband and a home of my own. Soon after I promised to love, honor, and obey, however, I discovered that this marriage did not resolve my loneliness after all. Nor did a home with children . . . three sons in the first four years only added to my inner need!

When I was twenty-seven, that inner need became a spiritual quest, leading me to a personal revelation of a new relationship with Jesus Christ. *But it took a horse . . . the training, in fact, of a headstrong young mare . . . to open the door to a new world that began to nourish my lonely spirit.* God used that world to teach me new insight on relationships and connection and on the value of that dreaded phenomenon of submission. In time, I found a personal vision of submission's role in a partnership.

My years of growing up were haunted by a mother's absence. My loneliness was magnified by a family conspiracy of silence on any details of explanation. I felt isolated and abandoned . . . and scared that something was wrong with me. *One's early heartaches, however, cannot be cured simply by becoming joined to another imperfect human being with heartaches of his own!* For years I struggled to find a closer relationship with my husband, while he told me to be satisfied with what we had. Marriage counselors advised me that Wes could not provide what I wanted. "You can accept him as he is, or you can leave," one told me. Something was better than nothing, we decided, so I stayed. I was afraid to venture out alone. My felt need for someone to help me was very real; I somehow lacked the assurance and courage to make it on my own. I had been too protected, perhaps, as a child.

After fourteen years of struggling and hoping for more, I got a horse! Actually, my husband bought Fanny for our oldest son, knowing that I'd wanted a horse all my life. Practical man that he was, he assumed I could share this horse with

Mark and be satisfied. *My passion for a horse could not be quenched, however, by anything less than exclusive ownership.* Three years later, Fanny was mine alone and I finally possessed not only the full enjoyment, but also the full responsibility. It was a humbling experience!

A man, I'm told, often retreats to a silent place to deal with his issues alone. *But a woman often needs to talk things out with a willing partner to help her find her way.* I seemed to feel that need more than most. I was always running to friends, to my dad, to ministers or counselors . . . perhaps because I couldn't talk to my husband about my problems or feelings. He was always busy, and he didn't want to talk about anything unpleasant. He didn't like to talk about much of anything, especially horses. Once he told me, "I shouldn't have to deal with your problems. I have enough of my own!" My feelings of being abandoned and isolated were only magnified.

A woman needs a relationship with intimate sharing and loving acceptance . . . a place of safety and belonging for her true self to emerge. The experience of training Fanny, combined with a special friendship with her new trainer, was life-changing. Alone with my horse, I felt I could finally be myself. The horse and rider experience satisfied my inner hunger more than any part of my marriage! A horse certainly can't offer wise counsel to help solve a woman's problems, but a listening ear is always supportive, even a long, hairy one! And my experiences with Fanny and her response to my attention taught me many things about the complexities of partnership.

My heart was softened by the feel of her velvet nose reaching out with inquisitive friendship. Like the prince's kiss that awakened Snow White, Fanny's touch made me come alive. The sound of her welcoming whinny stirred within me an answer of joyous companionship. *When a horse is right for the owner, a precious bond . . . a very real form of love . . . emerges from the response of one to the other.* That bond grew as Fanny and I shared countless miles of trail. There were struggles and uncertainties along the way . . . many of them . . . but gradually, with the help of a sensitive and experienced new friend, I discovered the gift of partnership! I found a sense of connection that made me feel whole and alive! It was a priceless gift!

My love for horses began with Grandpa Moats. If such an inclination is hereditary, he and his father passed it down to me. If not, it came through the influence of his stories about the horses he had owned and trained, and from my own childish reverence for a special grandpa. He was a great storyteller, and I listened eagerly when he talked about Peter Lincoln, Gyp, Brownie, and others that are now forgotten. My longing for a horse grew from a passionate childhood fantasy to a lifelong obsession.

As a toddler, I called him "Dompa" and followed him everywhere. I remember turning somersaults around a broom handle that he held across his knees. I asked him to cut my pancakes because I liked the way he did it. And I still love an evening snack of milk and crackers, because he did. He often sang to me at bedtime, but not the usual nursery rhymes! I remember two favorites: "There's a Long, Long Trail A-winding," and "The Preacher and the Bear." He sometimes brought ice cream or candy from town on Saturday nights. Now and then, he gave me a nickel, warning me with a grin not to spend it all in one place.

Grandpa was a blacksmith before he married and began farming. My old photos of him with his horses and the "Lyman E. Moats, Blacksmith" shop in Center Junction, Iowa, are among my most treasured keepsakes. I also have his antique hoof nippers and a pair of horseshoes he altered for a special purpose. He learned the trade from his father, Ambrose P. Moats, who was a blacksmith in the West Union area in the late 1800s before moving to Center Junction.

Grandpa was the traditional family patriarch. Dad didn't leave home when he married, but stayed to help with the farm. When I was three, Mother packed her suitcase, handed me to Grandma Bertha and walked out the door. After the divorce, I didn't see her again until I was twenty-seven. Like any woman, she wanted a home of her own, and there were too many conflicts between her and my grandparents. As I grew older, I had no memory of my mother. I was afraid to ask the questions that filled my wondering mind; Dad seemed angry for several years. His first mention of her that I remember was when I was twelve years old. Once, when I overslept, Grandpa's stern voice awakened me, "She's just like her mother; she'll never be worth a tap!" Grandma shushed him, but those words scarred my self-respect. Even after my reunion with Mother in 1966, our long and painful separation left a deep sense of loneliness and guilt that never fully healed. Dad never remarried.

Grandpa and I loved horse races. Whenever I watched a race, however, I would turn my head to hide my face, sure that no one would understand my reaction. I couldn't explain it then, but as I watched the tremendous power and beauty of those horses racing toward the finish line, I would get so caught up in the effort that I had to hold my breath and swallow hard. Even then, I couldn't stop the choking surge of emotion that swelled up from within, overflowing in actual tears of empathetic triumph as the winning horse crossed the finish line. *Was it possibly an expression of my own desire to win?*

"Someday we'll get you a horse," Grandpa had said, "soon as I find the right one." For some reason, that horse never crossed his path . . . and I was crucially disappointed. Perhaps he never felt any were good enough . . . but I'm sure he did look.

I remember vividly the day Wally Oldfather, a neighbor, rode over on his new black gelding. I lay on Grandpa and Grandma's bed, watching out their window as Wally and Grandpa talked, and I cried. *I wanted a horse of my own so very much.*

Grandpa always had a work team, and I could at least enjoy them. From all of his stories, my favorite involved two mules that he owned when I was still a toddler. He sold the mules at a farm sale in Scotch Grove, Iowa, when I was five years old. Grandpa said that people didn't bid on the mules because they were quite spirited and people were afraid of them. Those people didn't know how well-trained Grandpa's mules were!

23

I knew, because I sometimes led Jack and Jim to the water tank after a day's work. Grandpa loved to tell how I'd stub my toe and fall down. I'd scramble up quickly (while the mules stood and waited patiently) and I'd shake my little fist at the mules, loudly warning them, "You better behave, or I break every bone in your body!" I guess they were afraid of me, because they always behaved. I actually don't remember such spunky bravado, but Grandpa told the story many times, so it must have been so.

We moved to Montana and farmed for three years near Billings, and Grandpa bought a team of Belgian mares. I don't remember the mares or their names, but each had a colt, and I named the colts Meatball and Prince. The first time my cousin Joanne came to visit, I took her on a tour of our new farm. Meatball was lying in the small feedlot by the barn and I went over and climbed up on him. He got up and I slid off. At the time, Meatball was probably less than a year old and I was six. I can't remember if I ever told the folks about my brief ride, but I'm sure Joanne probably tattled!

It was in Montana, on my Uncle Kent's ranch near Roundup, that I actually rode a horse for the first time. Uncle Kent had a spotted Shetland pony mare, Babe, and I was allowed to ride one day during a family visit.

We moved back to Iowa to a 160 acre farm, and Grandpa bought two dapple-gray Percherons. Bell and Doll were a matched team with very different temperaments! Bell moved slower and needed a slap of the reins to keep up with Doll, who was nervous and eager. When I was older, I drove the Percherons while pulling a wagon, and sometimes on the hay rake. During the summer, we put hay into the barn loft using a big hayfork to lift it up out of the wagon. I led quiet, reliable Bell up the driveway from the barn as she pulled each heavy forkload by a pulley system into the barn. I had to be careful while turning around and coming back to the starting point to keep from being stepped on by her huge feet. She weighed about sixteen hundred pounds.

One special day, though I was wearing a dress, Grandpa lifted me up on Bell after a day's work and I rode her to the water tank. She didn't seem to mind; so after that, I rode quite often. I found an old bit in the barn and I braided twine to make a bridle and reins. Sometimes I used her harness bridle. I usually rode bareback, or sometimes I sat on an old rug tied around her with more braided twine. She was a good riding horse except for one irritating habit. If I leaned to one side to look at something, she would step sideways very quickly and I would usually slide off. She seemed almost proud of herself, while I scolded and sputtered and looked for a stump or fence to climb up on so I could get back on her!

My favorite place to ride was a dirt road through our forty acres of wooded pasture. I often sang as I rode and I knew most of the songs of Roy Rogers and The Sons of the Pioneers and Gene Autry by heart. Even then, in grade school, I felt a reverence for God and I sometimes pretended Jesus rode with me. I probably felt safer. Going after the cows was my favorite task, a search which sometimes took us up a steep hillside. I had to grab Bell's mane and hang on tight as she forged upward.

Sometime in my late teen years or early 20s, someone gave me a book by Dale Evans and Roy Rogers, *The Answer Is God*. That book had a great influence on my own search for life's questions and answers. Raised as an only child, without many friends my age, I saw life more seriously than most kids. I spent a lot of time in our woods, riding or walking with my dog, thinking, meditating, and praying.

Bell was my special friend. I often sat in her feed bunk as she munched the hay in her manger. I combed her mane and told her all my problems and dreams. She listened quietly and never laughed or criticized. For several years, Bell was the closest I came to having a horse of my own. Until Fanny came along.

The circumstances that brought Fanny convinced me that God had finally heard my life-long prayers. *And maybe Grandpa's promise just took longer to accomplish because it had to be God's timing!*

I know Grandpa Moats would have liked Fanny. He favored horses with spirit and energy, and Fanny had plenty of both. I strongly wished he was still around to help train her. Fortunately, God sent someone else to help with Fanny's training, a woman who became a special friend.

Along the way, God gave me much more than the mere joy of owning a horse. He taught me profound lessons that I might not have learned any other way . . . about horses, about myself, and about relationships. *There is a spiritual message in the horse and rider experience . . . and sharing that message is the purpose of my writing.* Through my special bond with Fanny, God revealed His desire for an intimate relationship with me . . . and I slowly grew to understand how that relationship works best. As I sensed His unconditional love and His Fatherly wisdom and protection, I came to understand that a woman's greatest need is not for a husband, a close friend, or a horse, but for the ultimate connection and partnership with her Creator!

CHAPTER 2

A Place of Belonging

Fanny was a headstrong mare, with the challenge and anticipation of one's first horse that no other will ever match. She wasn't that great looking, she was ornery much of the time, and she was never as submissive as I wished she could have been. She freely expressed her own indomitable spirit and reacted to frightful surroundings with intimidating strength. She was an exciting companion with special vigor . . . and she was mine. In spite of what Fanny was or was not, she tried to please me. We truly had something precious in the relationship that developed from our struggles and trials.

Her whinny always greeted me as I entered the barn. *When I put my arms around her neck, snuggling into its substantial warmth, I found my place of belonging.* Riding the trails, I felt braver because she was carrying me. She lifted me above my earthly existence . . . far away from the misery of a life that was never quite what I wanted. Fanny helped me find a freedom of spirit in which to soar for a time.

She would stand in the pasture, like a statue of polished mahogany gleaming in the summer sun, ears pricked forward, head high. She would turn her head from side to side as if looking for some awful thing behind her . . . some excuse to bolt. And when it was seen, she would arch her neck and whirl, snorting and blowing, running her own private race with an unseen rival. Now and then it was a stiff-legged canter, with tail up and mane flying, nostrils flaring and that loud blowing through her nose . . . that explosive snort. Sometimes it was a prancy trot with head tucked and neck beautifully arched, hooves reaching out with great extension and that exquisite momentary hesitation and suspension in the air between pogo-stick landings. That was my favorite.

I loved to watch Fanny's performances. The dishes would go unwashed, the floor unswept, the laundry undone while I stood at the window, watching until she went back to calmly eating grass and I knew the show was over.

That was my Fanny . . . an energetic, head-strong mare with a free-spirited nature. Others noticed a cantankerous gleam in her small red-rimmed eyes, or saw her heavy neck and unre-fined head, and a lack of perfect conformation. I saw her remarkable spirit.

Fifteen years later, Fanny carried little girls on her back with tender care. But even with a shoulder injury, she ran with abandon when turned out to pasture with other horses. *And none better question her position as lead mare!* Protectively aggressive, Fanny quickly estab-lished her place at the top of the pecking order. She would run at other horses with ears back and teeth bared, and she would whirl and kick. And that's exactly what led to her death when she was twenty.

For sixteen years, she was my escape, my comfort, and my obsession. I wanted to prove to the world that she really had the greatness that I saw in her. I wanted her to win some-thing! *I realized later that it was my own need for identity and self-worth that drove me in this obsession.* I wanted to do whatever it took to make her live up to my hopeful dreams, but Fanny and I were both limited by my own posi-tion in my human family. Unlike Fanny, I had never been a "lead mare."

Although Fanny meant a great deal to me, the attention I gave her created strong conflict with my husband. Counselors advised me to sell my horse and concentrate on being a more submissive wife and a better mother. It wasn't that simple. I followed my doctor's advice . . . to ride as much as possible as a way of dealing with the stress.

I hadn't asked my husband to buy a place in the country, but I was happy when he announced that we were buying a place with four acres and a big house and barn. He had been transferred to Springfield, Illinois, and he had found this little homestead near Loami, about fifteen miles west of the capitol city.

At the closing, he said, "Maybe now you can have that horse you've always wanted." Did he really mean it? Though my desire to own a horse had been pushed aside my whole life until then, it had definitely not been forgotten. It was merely waiting for that soft nose and a whinny to bring it to life. We'd been busy raising three boys and moving every few years while Wes stepped up the employment ladder to higher income. There hadn't been a place or time for a horse until now.

After fourteen years in the suburbs, I was back in the country! Our new home was spacious and old, a partly remodeled farmhouse that needed a lifetime of more work. There was a big old red barn with no stalls inside, but there was plenty of room to build several. And there were almost four acres that could be fenced for pasture. I had high hopes that here at last, someday, I could have my horse!

My anticipation was soon discouraged, however. In spite of my hopes, our country place was more for the boys than for Mom's horse. As much as I wanted that horse, we didn't buy Fanny for me; we bought her for our twelve-year-old son, Mark, for his 4-H project. Our sons were almost teenagers. Wes decided they needed to be in 4-H and he encouraged each one to choose a project. We had both grown up on farms and been active in 4-H. It was one of the few things we agreed on—that 4-H would be good for the boys at their age.

David, our youngest, wanted a flock of chickens. Before we were through, we were taking care of two hundred White Leghorn hens, selling dozens of fresh eggs, and even filling our freezer with fresh meat. Butchering a couple dozen fat hens was not my favorite thing. We only did that when Wes' parents came to visit. They had more experience with the details of the task and less problem doing it.

Bob chose a registered Holstein cow named June. After a few years, we had a small herd.

Mark, our oldest, later bought his own cow, Babe, who did her share to add to the business. I was amazed that one cow could give four gallons at one milking (Dad's shorthorns had never given that much)! We sold milk and cream and had plenty to drink and use. I made my own butter now and then and sometimes cottage cheese and yogurt.

Above all, I remember the night that one young cow gave birth to her first calf. The boys all went to bed, letting nature take its course, not worrying about any problems. Wes must have been out of town that night. I went out and checked on things every hour or so, growing more and more concerned with the proceedings . . . or lack of. Finally, when two little hooves were showing for too long without further results, I called our vet. He agreed that he needed to come. It was a June night, clear and warm, with generous moonlight. Two vets arrived sometime around midnight and tried to "pull" the calf without success. I can't remember if it was my idea or the vet's, but I finally drove our old Ford pickup around to the pasture. We hooked a chain around the calf's hooves and I inched ahead, slowly and carefully. It worked! The big calf was almost blue from his long ordeal, and Mom was pretty miserable, but both survived.

After the vets left, I stood alone awhile in the warm, cozy darkness, savoring the experience, reliving each detail. *I felt a deep sense of thankfulness in the sacred miracle of life and my own small part in helping to save two animals.*

Standing there, I remembered a hot summer day when I was a teenager driving our team of Percherons on the hay rake. I could smell the sweat of the horses that day and I stopped them for a brief rest at the shady edge of the field. As they stood there, breathing hard and switching flies with their tails, I looked down into the valley below our farm, where a hawk circled slowly. Sitting there on the metal seat of the old hay rake, alone in the field with the two horses, I felt a profound sense of humble dependence and belonging to the land that supported us, a moment of insight I will never forget.

The folks worked hard to live off our farm. We had pigs, chickens, cows and the team of horses. We gathered eggs every day and milked the cows. We had a big garden and several fruit trees. Grandma canned vegetables and fruits from the garden to eat year round. We picked berries from the woods. We planted crops to feed our animals.

God gave us sun and rain and we usually had a good harvest. We always had food to eat and we didn't have any debts. Perhaps I matured a bit that day in the field with the horses, as I genuinely understood the humble, thankful attitude I saw in my folks. *We depended on God.* And when times were difficult, Grandpa would say, "Things will work out. He's always taken care of us in the past. We'll take the bad with the good."

I appreciated my family heritage . . . the background that created and nurtured my passion for horses, my love of the country, and my reverence for God. I wanted our new country home to somehow provide the same for our boys. But things were different here.

CHAPTER 3

A Horse for Mark

Before Mark bought his Holstein cow, he wanted a horse for his first 4-H project. And I couldn't wait to help him find one! He was twelve and he had ridden on a few trail rides. He should have gotten a well-trained, older horse to begin with, but I didn't even consider the more expensive horses. Years later, I realized Wes spent almost three times as much on each cow, choosing the best quality bloodlines. Yet I thought we couldn't afford a good horse. Was it my own Scotch attitude . . . or my lack of confidence? Or was it some kind of family belief that cows are worth more than horses? I can't help but wonder . . . if I had found a good expensive horse, would Wes have bought it?

Circumstances, however, seemed to lead in a certain direction. When we first moved to Loami, I met a neighbor who sold my brand of make-up and listened to my tale of woes. It was mushroom season and I was restless. I was doing some freelance advertising and I needed the help of an artist. I was looking for a friend . . . and a horse. "You've got to meet Helen Kyle!" said my neighbor with a knowing nod. And she took me over and introduced me.

Helen was an artist who lived two miles from me, on the edge of town, with a creek, wildflowers, mushrooms, and two horses that weren't being ridden.

Honey had been trained and shown as their daughter's 4-H project at one time, but Patricia was married now and didn't ride anymore. I fell in love with Honey, just watching her running in the pasture. She was seven years old, Helen said, and her filly was four . . . that was Fanny.

Honey and Fanny both were a dark liver chestnut, each with different markings. Honey had a white blaze and three white stockings; Fanny had a star and one white sock. Both stood about 15 1/2 hands tall. Honey had better conformation. Fanny was halter broke and they had been on her a few times, but she wasn't yet trained to ride. Honey had been trained to obey word commands, which impressed me.

I couldn't help but admire Honey's independent spirit. *Isn't one reason we love horses because we feel stirred deep inside by their magnificent beauty as they move and run?* We want to "own" their strength and their sense of freedom.

"Why aren't you doing something with these horses?" I would ask Helen. "It's such a waste!" But she said they enjoyed just having them around, feeding them apples over the fence. I knew if I owned two horses that they would be ridden every day! But then, I still hadn't owned horses and I had a lot to learn.

Mark and I looked for his horse, but everything seemed too expensive. I'd call about an ad, and then I'd go ride the horse. I'd ask questions and learn what I could. I didn't find anything I really liked . . . and I always came back to Honey and Fanny. Helen said they weren't for sale, but we did talk now and then about the possibility. Wes thought Mark could use Honey for his 4-H project while I trained Fanny. We finally agreed that I could work with Honey to see if we really wanted her.

I'd go over with a handful of apples just so I could catch and brush her. It usually took half an hour of coaxing with grain and apples to get close enough to put a rope around her neck. I must admit I was sometimes frustrated beyond words, but I was also challenged by the need to win the trust of this elusive mare!

Meanwhile, Fanny would be right there getting in my way, wanting the treats. *Such a pest,* I thought. I shooed her away and went after Honey. But Honey would toss her head and gallop off across the pasture. I thrilled at Honey's agile speed and spirited nature. *Did I fail to see the untamed look in her eye?*

Working Honey on a lunge line for a few weeks, I found her to be well-trained and intelligent. I decided it was time to ride her. Since Honey worked on word commands, we tied a rope to her halter instead of using a bridle. Helen's husband helped me put their saddle on her, and I climbed aboard eagerly while our three boys watched from behind the fence. I said "walk" and Honey walked. I asked for a trot, and she trotted. I said, "canter," and off she cantered, smooth and easy. *This is great,* I thought.

Then I asked for the trot again. Instead of obeying, she tossed her head, lowered it, and showed me a part of her nature that I had previously missed! Her easy canter got faster as she headed for a thicket of trees at the edge of the pasture. I pulled harder on the halter rope. As she ran under the branches, I ducked my head. I had just had my hair done the day before, in a beautifully curled "beehive" type hairdo. Honey definitely had no respect for my beautician's efforts, I thought, as I felt the hairpins flying.

Inside the thicket of small trees was a tiny clearing, then a fence. Honey stopped suddenly at the fence, then whirled around and went back out under the tree branches. I ducked again. So far, I was too proud of staying on to be scared of the alternative. But fear was slowly creeping into my more sensible consciousness! I had never ridden a horse of this nature before and I really didn't know quite what to do.

Honey ran down the pasture slope, heading straight for an old bridge floor that had been dragged up against a tree. Not having any control, I remember wondering if I could manage to jump off. Honey didn't wait. Bill told me later that she was bucking as she ran. I flipped over in the air, landing on the back of my neck, stunned for a moment. Our three sons had watched from behind the fence, and I'm sure Mark was beginning to worry about having Honey as his 4-H project. Bill said I ought to get back on her, but I told him I had to wait until my head cleared.

"She can't get away with that," Bill declared as he got on. But before I could join the boys at the fence, Bill landed up against it with his shirt caught on the barbed wire. I noticed his back was scratched under his torn shirt. Without a word, he went to the house.

Honey stood still, quite calm after what she had done, and she let me walk up to her and take hold of her halter rope. A moment later, Bill returned with a bridle. With a bit in her mouth, Honey behaved much better and Bill rode a few minutes while I rested. I rode her again for a short time after my head cleared, but only at a walk. I could sense the tightness in her muscles at the point where she ran away with me and I didn't want to take chances! Following my chiropractor's orders, I didn't ride again for a long time.

In spite of my experience with Honey, we went ahead and signed an agreement to buy both horses, paying installments over several months. The knock on our kitchen door early next Saturday morning brought disappointing news, yet I was relieved without wanting to admit it. This was the very morning when we were to get the two horses. When I opened the door, Helen was obviously embarrassed, and apologetic, but she quickly told us they had just sold Honey to someone else!

Honey had not been advertised for sale. Yet this family had come with a trailer, she explained, and insisted on buying her. They paid cash, she said, twice as much as we had agreed to pay for her. Who were these people? Helen didn't know them. They were from a small town about an hour's drive away. Why did they want Honey? Helen didn't know. But they offered too good a price, in cash, to turn down, she said. And we could still have Fanny. Helen's story sounded very convincing.

Whatever really happened, I thank God for His merciful help in the matter. I didn't object too loudly. Some people later told us Honey was a real outlaw, and I'm thankful we didn't get her. I must admit that I always wondered what really happened to Honey, but I never questioned Helen about the truth of her story. We had grown to be good friends, and I actually believed that Helen had our best interests in mind. We agreed to go ahead and buy Fanny for Mark's 4-H project.

CHAPTER 4

Fanny Comes Home

We brought Fanny home in December of 1974, on a warm Saturday afternoon. Sitting in the open trunk of our Honda Accord, I held her lead rope as Wes drove slowly over two miles of blacktop. It worked for us at the time, but I would never recommend that method of moving a horse.

Alone in a strange pasture, away from her mother for the first time, Fanny ran the fence line for days, making a muddy track. Everyone else went about their business, but I worried that Fanny could get loose or hurt herself. It soon became a habit to stand at the window, watching her, instead of doing housework. *The more I watched, the more I liked the pest I once shooed away*. Fanny was not as beautifully put together as her mother, and fortunately not as treacherous. She had her own spirited nature and she was mischievously ornery, quite headstrong, and very excitable. And she was ours.

Sometime early that next spring, my husband came into the house with a disgusted look and a brief announcement; "Your horse is out . . . you can go catch her!"

"How on earth did she get loose?" I asked as I grabbed a jacket . . . even though she wasn't really MY horse.

"She somehow got the barn door open," he replied. "And I'm not going to catch her." I knew I was the best person for that job and was out the door in seconds.

Fanny's barn was actually an old corncrib. One end had a door while the other end opened into a small acre of fenced pasture. The rest of our property was mostly grass, surrounded partially by an old fence on one side and the neighbor's plowed ground. Fanny could have run for miles without anything stopping her. But there she was, racing joyfully around on our four acres.

I knew better than to chase her. I headed for the barn to get some grain, walking along the fence line and calling her as I walked. Halfway to the barn, I saw that she had stopped and was

46

watching me. I called her again and she tossed her head and came running straight at me.

The sight of this charging equine was a bit frightening, but the fence was directly behind me. I stood still, sure she'd stop before running over me. Sure enough, she slid to a halt directly in front of me and I reached up and grabbed her halter. She whirled to run away, actually swinging me off my feet for a moment because I did not let go. When she realized I still held her, she stopped with her head high, snorting.

I led her back to the barn, as she continued to prance and snort. As I neared the open door, she pulled away and ran inside. How easily she could have run the opposite direction to enjoy her freedom once again. She knew where she belonged!

One way or another, Fanny managed to get loose about once a month. She would unlatch the corncrib door, unfasten the pasture gate, or break down the old fence. She would kick up her heels and run and buck and prance and snort, usually staying on our own property. After she'd had her fun, she would let me catch her. It was obviously all a game, which frustrated our whole family and probably delighted her to no end!

Later, when we put up a hot wire to enclose all of our pasture, she seemed more content. I watched several times, however, as she purposefully charged through the hot wire, usually to enjoy the greener grass of our front yard. Sometimes she broke through to join a horse and rider that passed by on the road . . . but most riders didn't seem to appreciate her company and they usually didn't come by again.

We started from the beginning with Fanny's training, as though she had never been ridden. She didn't want to stand still to be saddled or bridled, and I was careful to keep my feet out of her way. I lunged her at first and Mark and I both worked with her until she accepted being ridden. She never bucked or reared with us during her training.

Helen told us that Fanny had been ridden a few times, but didn't like a bit. "You might want to start with a hackamore," she suggested.

"Why would you use a hackamore?" an older horseman asked me. "I'll sell you a bit for five dollars that will give you better control."

After my experience with Honey, control sounded good. I learned much later that this particular bit was too small for her mouth and much too severe. It was a terrible bit to start with! No wonder Fanny opened her mouth and threw her head up as Mark pulled on the reins!

Mark's inexperienced hands were not gentle and light. He pulled on the reins a lot, because

Fanny was always wanting to go faster. How I wish I had known then what I know now. We should have started with a different bit and spent more time teaching her to accept it. The mistakes we made early in Fanny's training were never totally corrected.

That same old horseman who sold me the bit also asked me why I would buy "that nag." He said he wanted to come watch when I tried to load her into a horse trailer the first time, so he could have a good laugh. Actually, she got into the back of our pickup truck with stock racks with very little trouble. I simply backed into a ditch, putting the back end of the truck against higher ground. Then I coaxed her in with an ear of corn. It took only a few minutes for her to decide she wanted to follow the corn!

Later, after I bought a real horse trailer, the old horseman would have had his laugh on several occasions. I was glad he wasn't around.

Even though I'd grown up around horses with a grandfather who knew about horses, that didn't automatically give me the knowledge and skill I needed to train Fanny. My husband assumed I could handle it. Fanny weighed eleven hundred to twelve hundred pounds and she was built heavy. I was told she had some thoroughbred in her, and her temperament seemed to match. She was headstrong, eager, easily spooked, and sometimes difficult to control.

It helped to remember some of Grandpa's horse stories. "Never walk up behind a horse without talking to him," was one rule drilled into my head. Grandma Moats lost her father when she was very young because he forgot. I always remembered to speak to Fanny when approaching her from behind.

I attended 4-H meetings with Mark and talked to the leaders. I asked questions of anyone who would take time to answer. I read magazines, trying to learn everything I could about horse training.

Mark managed for three years to ride Fanny in 4-H events and around home without getting hurt. She did quite well in halter class, even though she did not want to stand square. One judge placed her seventh in a string of twenty horses, commenting that she was not "turned out" as well as she could be. We didn't even understand what he meant. We didn't realize how important grooming, trimming, and conditioning were. She did look kind of ragged, compared to the other "beauties" in the show.

In Western Pleasure classes, while other horses tucked their heads and trotted slowly, Fanny was constantly nodding her head and pulling at the reins, wanting to pass them all. A tight rein only made her pull and nod more.

Mark decided Fanny had a better calling. "I'm going to race her," he announced. I objected strongly. "But didn't they say in the 4-H meetings that you shouldn't race a horse until after she's been trained for pleasure riding? You'll ruin her!"

My husband agreed that Fanny should be good for something. So Mark put her in every plug race, barrel race, catalog race, or flag race he could manage. He couldn't do the poles, since Fanny didn't know her leads. She never won first, but she always came in second, third, fourth or fifth. Mark soon had a shoebox full of ribbons.

Once, I remember Mark coming off unexpectedly when Fanny went through an open gate instead of circling inside the arena. Luckily, he wasn't hurt.

Even with the ribbons, Fanny still lacked good training. I watched Mark ride and I tried to help. "Keep your heels down," I reminded him. "Sit up straight. Relax your hands." I was always "encouraging" him to ride, and I was often frustrated that he would ride only a few minutes before putting Fanny back out to pasture.

I kept telling myself that Fanny was Mark's project and her training was supposed to be his responsibility. I helped all I could, but how would he learn if he didn't do more on his own? I ached to handle Fanny myself, more than just riding her now and then down the road with my friends. Why didn't he work more with her? Why didn't he want to improve her performance? She had so much potential . . . didn't he understand? Didn't he care? Didn't he know what to do?

When Mark turned fifteen, school events, cars, and girls were occupying much more of his time than his horse. With my husband's encouragement, Fanny was bred and "Little War Dude" was born April 15, 1977. A blue roan with white blanket, just like his daddy, Dude was definitely an Appaloosa! Now Mark had two horses, and I found myself being even more of a nag about Fanny's need for care and exercise.

One day, I decided I had to back off. Feeling very guilty, I sat down and wrote out my feelings in a farewell to Fanny, saying in effect "You are not mine. You belong to Mark and I will let go." Soon afterward, however, everything changed!

Perhaps in hopes of finding peace as much as anything, Mark and his Dad decided to give Mom a bill of sale for Fanny as a birthday present. *So in September of 1977, on my thirty-eighth birthday, Fanny was officially mine! I finally had my dream . . . a horse of my very own!*

CHAPTER 5

Search for a Trainer

For three years, I had tried to help Mark train his horse. Now Fanny was mine, an answer to a lifelong dream . . . *and I finally had to face a humbling truth.* I was intimidated by her energy and strength and I didn't know how to get her under control for Mark's sake or my own! Had I wanted Mark to do something I couldn't do myself?

How often we set our minds in a certain direction and fail to see the truth about ourselves . . . until some challenging reality comes along to wake us up to a new perspective! Too often, we cannot acknowledge our weakness until it is too apparent to deny . . . and too often we refuse to recognize our real need.

About that time, I saw something that grew to have a great impact later on my life. I had watched horse shows before, with well-dressed riders and polished horses competing for prizes. But one afternoon, I happened to observe a young woman dressed in jeans and tee shirt schooling a gray Arabian in an empty Coliseum.

Round and round, the pair circled the vast arena at a steady trot. I stopped to watch, fascinated at the consistent rhythmic movement. His head tucked obediently, ears forward and alert, the Arab trotted briskly in unbroken cadence. There was no wasted motion, no turning or nodding of his head, no pulling at the bit and no stumbling or wandering in any direction. In complete cooperation with his rider, he moved like a graceful machine, maintaining the same collected energetic stride the entire time that I watched. I found myself caught up in the graceful "oneness" of horse and rider.

She rode English. I marveled at how quietly she sat, her hands and feet steady as she posted, with only her headscarf bobbing gently. Here was a simple demonstration of the essence of good riding and the ideal relationship of horse and rider without the distraction of showy costumes and fancy braids. It was the first time I noticed how natural the English way of riding could be . . . and how different from the way I rode!

Fanny was definitely not as well trained as the Arab in the Coliseum, and I was definitely not as skilled as that young woman riding him. I loved to ride Fanny on our country roads with my friends, but her lack of training was apparent. She was a bundle of energy not waiting for direction. She fought the bit and threw her head up and down. Her trot was bouncy and inconsistent in rhythm and direction. She seemed to be always looking for something that might get her. She often spooked at anything that moved or made a noise, including cows, cats, dogs, pigs, or weeds!

I was glad I rode Western; I needed all the help I could get to stay in the saddle. One minute Fanny would be walking down the middle of the road; the next minute she could leap in any direction. It became an automatic reflex to grab hold with my legs whenever she leaped and I was proud of myself for staying on her. She eagerly pranced and snorted and I enjoyed the adventure of each ride on this energetic, spirited mare.

After watching the young woman and the Arab, however, I realized the advantages and effects of good training and manners. How I wished I could ride with more skill, to be able to train Fanny to be that well behaved! *I never knew the woman's name, but from that day on she was my inspiration to learn greater riding skills.*

I didn't believe Fanny would ever accept that kind of control, or that I could ever have the discipline that English riding required. I wanted to do so much more with Fanny, but I just didn't have the skill or the knowledge to train her further. As much as I hated to admit it, I finally told my husband that I wanted help.

"Let me take her to a professional trainer. Just one month," I begged. "It will cost a couple hundred, but then she'll be safer to ride." Wes was reluctant at first, but I persisted and he finally agreed. I knew Fanny had potential; she just needed the right handling to bring it out and I couldn't do it. A trainer would have an indoor arena and could start earlier in the year. I couldn't start serious riding until April because of the weather, and I figured the trainer would have her under control by then. I hoped one month would be enough.

In January of 1978, I chose a trainer who agreed to work with Fanny, starting in February. When I called to make final arrangements, however, he asked me to wait a month, since his assistant had broken her arm. When I called again, about the first of March, he told me to "come ahead, we're ready for her." But when I called the company that rented horse trailers, a company I had used several times before, I was told they had just sold their trailers and quit the rental business.

It took me another month to locate a trailer. I asked every horse owner I knew until I found one willing to help me. Before anything could be done, however, we had a major ice storm. Every utility pole on our road snapped from the weight of power lines encased in heavy layers of ice, leaving us without electricity for thirteen days.

One pole fell across our driveway, and we had to park on the road by the edge of the garden for almost two weeks. But finally the poles and lines were cleared away and I could hardly wait to load Fanny up and take her to the trainer. He was ready for her and I had a trailer to get her there. It was time to start the old pickup truck and get going.

But now the old pickup wouldn't start. We tried jumper cables, but that didn't work. My husband checked every possibility he could think of. He cleaned the battery posts. He checked wires and connections. Nothing helped.

"I think it's going to be a while before you drive this truck," he told me.

It was two more weeks and well into April by the time we got the pickup running. The weather was nice enough by now to ride outdoors regularly. I had been so excited about putting Fanny with a professional trainer; I believed it was the answer to all my problems! For three months, however, one delay after another had postponed my dream. I was frustrated beyond words, but I decided that there had to be a reason for the delays. *I was beginning to believe that I was not meant to take Fanny to this trainer!*

"Lord, I give up," I told Him. "You seem to be preventing my plans. But You know how much I need help! What do I do now?"

My answer came only a few days later. I was at work when a young woman entered the office and introduced herself to the receptionist. Hearing her name, I knew she wrote a weekly newspaper column that I read faithfully. While she waited for her appointment, I told her how much I enjoyed her writing. We talked a few minutes and I learned she had horses, so I told her about my efforts to take Fanny to a trainer.

Pam's response was an emphatic, "You should train her yourself!"

"I've always wanted to do that," I told her, "but I don't know how to go any further." Three years of helping Mark had convinced me how little I really knew!

"I'll help you."

I had heard those words before, several times. And the help I had received hadn't been much or the kind I wanted. I was afraid to count on someone I didn't even know. But Pam said she could come on Friday, which was my day off, so I agreed. It was noon when she finished her appointment, and she suggested we go out for lunch and talk some more. Half way through her bowl of hot soup, Pam paused a moment. "You're different. You know Jesus Christ, don't you?" She glanced up at me, not questioningly but with a knowing look.

I nodded. "Yes, I do. And you?"

"I have a deep faith in God," she replied, without further explanation.

Had God really sent this woman to help me train Fanny? Would she be able to do more than the professional trainer I had originally chosen? Or was I hoping for too much?

Dear Lord, help us to face the truth about ourselves . . . our weakness and our need. Help us to see the Truth of Your love and mercy, Your wisdom and power, and Your Sovereign control! And help us to respond in submission to Your wise and compassionate leadership so that our lives might be stronger, better, and more complete!

CHAPTER 6

"Train Her Yourself!"

*P*am came that Friday, as she had promised, bringing her friend, Bob, with her. They looked Fanny over thoroughly and asked several questions about her history. I remember Pam asking Bob, "Do you think she's worth the effort?" His answer wasn't eagerly positive, but Pam seemed satisfied.

"I was meant to see into your heart," she later confided. "And I saw the same spirit in Fanny's eyes that my own mare had." What she had seen in me and Fanny was a possibility of what she herself had experienced with a beloved mare and she was willing to try to give us that special relationship.

Her first recommendation was a different feeding program. Fanny's first colt, Dude, was a year old now. I thought we were giving both horses plenty to eat, but with Fanny's winter hair shed off, her ribs were more evident than I'd ever seen them!

"I don't like to ride a horse this thin," Pam told me. "Give her exercise on the lunge line for a few weeks and increase her feed."

I had been feeding oats in summer and corn in winter, just like Grandpa Moats gave his work teams. Following Pam's suggestion, I bought sweet feed and mixed it with oats and whole corn. Pam believed that whole kernel corn helped keep a horse's teeth in better shape. Normally, a horse's teeth grow and develop sharp edges that can irritate the mouth while eating or holding a bit. The teeth need to be "floated" regularly, which means a veterinarian or equine dentist grinds the sharp edges off with a rasp.

I'd had Fanny's teeth floated once when she was five, and the vet recommended floating at least once a year. But after whole corn was added to her feed, Fanny didn't seem to need floating again, even when she was twenty years old. Maybe I was just lucky!

Pam convinced me that good nutrition, health, and soundness were of primary importance before beginning any training program. I not only increased and changed the feed mix, I took more care to choose good quality hay without mold or dust, preferably a grass-alfalfa mix. During the three years that Mark owned Fanny, we'd had several bad experiences with colic. It could have been the hay, our lack of worming, or something entirely different. But once I added a handful of wet wheat bran to her grain on a regular basis, we had no more problems with colic.

Pam returned a few weeks later to check on our progress. Fanny's weight was better and Pam agreed we were ready to begin serious training. Even after lunging Fanny, I was nervous and excited as I saddled her. Pam first had me ride Fanny while she held the lunge line. She saw how Fanny behaved and offered suggestions as I rode. Pam then unsnapped the line and I rode out alone into our small pasture . . . until Fanny acted up and started fighting the bit. Pam called us back, snapped the lunge line back on the bridle, and Fanny and I both calmed down.

Pam explained that returning to a familiar exercise is a basic training principle when problems appear. Problems often mean the horse does not understand what is expected, is nervous, or isn't ready to cooperate (in this case, it probably meant the rider needed lots of help!). Going back to something familiar was better than fighting, Pam believed . . . and I agreed!

Pam told me later that she noticed how my hands shook a little as I climbed into the saddle. She was careful to keep our training sessions under control. She didn't put me in a situation where I had to fight with Fanny. She taught me new ways to deal with each problem as we progressed in the training.

It would have been easier to train Fanny correctly as a young horse. She was eight years old now, and she had learned some bad habits that needed to be patiently restructured. She also had learned how to outsmart her human master. Pam had to correct Fanny and teach me at the same time.

For instance, Fanny had become quite a bully. Fanny didn't always neck rein if she didn't feel like it. When I tried to turn her by direct rein, she would bend her neck with my pull but keep going her own direction. Instead of pulling on her mouth, Pam suggested I slap her on the neck or use my hat. Since I often rode with a wide-brimmed Western straw hat, that method seemed quite convenient and actually worked wonders in Fanny's training! The results were well worth the price of a new hat!

Fanny was "bull-headed" in other ways as well. The first time I asked her to back up, she practically ran me down! Later, I asked her to back and she would do it, but not in a straight line. I remember the first time Pam asked her to back. When she started to go forward, Pam's loud scolding stopped her. And when she started to back crooked, Pam quickly showed her what she expected. No whips, no punishment, just a voice of authority and body language that told Fanny who was in charge. Watching Pam at work was an education in itself.

I soon realized I had more to learn about horse training than I thought! Returning periodically to check on my progress and offer new suggestions, Pam taught me about health care and horse psychology, physical therapy, handling and control, and about the horse/human relationship. I called her with problems as they occurred and Pam was generous with her knowledge.

She later shared how her equestrian education had begun when she was a young child. She had received excellent training and a lifetime of fantastic experiences. She knew the basics and more, and I was grateful for her coaching. It was a joy to work with someone who knew what to do. I never imagined anyone would be so willing to spend so much time helping me! I soon realized Pam had a special gift when it came to the relationship of horse and human. She and I had also found an exceptional friendship of our own through our mutual interest in Fanny's development.

"I like Fanny's spirit," Pam told me. "You could make her a well-trained machine, but you'd break her spirit and you don't want that. You want to win her willing cooperation."

Pam told me about the famous white Lipizzan stallions and how they are trained to perform at liberty. This was the kind of training I wanted for Fanny. Many people I had talked to lacked respect for a horse. "You've got to make her mind!" I'd been told. "Whip her into submission. Make her know you're the boss!" I didn't want to be that kind of horse trainer. I believed Fanny had the right to be treated with kind respect. And, at the risk of sounding corny, I loved her too much to be mean to her! But that attitude, together with my fear of her, is what had spoiled her!

I'm more aware now of the different methods that trainers use. Those who try to force new behavior sometimes get good results. Then the owner gets the horse back and old problems reoccur. That might have happened to me before I met Pam. Things go so much better when you patiently work with a horse yourself to develop a good relationship, to earn its trust and respect and the horse becomes willingly obedient. I'm glad more trainers now teach good communication and mutual respect.

I remembered Mark's frustration trying to teach Fanny to stand square for 4-H halter class. We took her to a trainer for help. That was Fanny's first time in a regular stall, in a strange place with many strange horses. She kicked, damaging one corner of the trainer's barn. She broke fences. She probably cost the trainer more that week than I paid for training. At the end of the week, I saw whip marks all over Fanny's chest and rump.

"You need to teach this horse discipline!" the trainer told me. I wasn't comfortable with the situation, so I took Fanny home. She was more excitable than ever. We had her fearful attention, but not her trust. *We had to start all over*.

I understand how fear of a horse's size and strength causes a need to control, but pain and force cause fear and a defensive instinct to fight back. Any quick hand movement can frighten a horse that's been whipped. I agreed with Pam that Fanny's energy and spirit needed firm control, not punishment. Pam knew what to do and she had the confidence to do it well. She was patient, consistent, and firm, and Fanny learned to trust and respect her leadership. Pam took control in order to teach Fanny how to obey.

"When you tame a horse," Pam told me, "that horse is always yours." She was referring to a horse's spirit yielding to its chosen master. Handled with patience and kind authority, a horse will learn to cooperate willingly, out of trust. Gaining Fanny's cooperation through trust and respect created a strong affectionate bond and a treasured partnership. She was also speaking of responsibility. Training Fanny the right way was very important to me. Pam understood, more than I did. I wanted desperately to make Fanny a winner. Pam saw my inner need for the relationship, and she had a desire to help.

Six weeks after Fanny's training began, Pam took Fanny to her own barn for a few months. Working at her convenience, she led Fanny around for hours, asking her to pay attention to her handler and look where she was going. Fanny was led over tree limbs and poles, up and down hills, over ditches, around anything handy. Pam didn't let Fanny charge ahead and take her own control. Fanny learned to follow, to be led, to let a human take control. For weeks, Pam worked in short, easy periods, several times each day. This was a huge challenge for Fanny and exhausting for Pam, but it was an essential foundation for all of Fanny's further training. Fanny needed to learn to work submissively with a human master.

Pam had taken Fanny from the pasture and put her in a stall again. Depending on a human for food and freedom, Fanny got a strong message concerning who was boss. Daily grooming and handling throughout each day helped Fanny accept human touch and authority. Although Fanny kicked the stall and leaned on fences, she didn't cause extensive damage.

Fanny basically wanted to please, and she got upset when scolded. She just couldn't seem to quiet down enough to be told what to do! *Pam had the patience to ask Fanny to wait, to listen, and to follow.* Pam rewarded the slightest effort with praise, but she also let Fanny know verbally when her headstrong behavior wasn't appreciated.

Fanny was often tied with a stout rope to a snubbing post. She learned she could not get free by pulling back, which she tried many times. Tying a horse that pulls back out of fear would only make matters worse. Fanny's pulling back was an aggressive desire for control and freedom and she needed to learn to accept being tied.

We "sacked her out," which involved tying her securely and carefully shaking a blanket all around her, touching her with the blanket until she learned to tolerate it and stand quietly. Pam also tied milk jugs to the saddle to get Fanny used to distractions.

Fanny needed to learn respect for human space. A sharp thumb applied to the ribs taught her it was bad manners to step on her owner's feet. When Fanny moved, however, she moved quickly, not always looking where she was going. Her body moved at times like an adolescent colt, and she sometimes stepped on her own feet.

A horse's feet are one of the most important considerations of all. Fanny had never worn shoes, and her hooves had spread. Pam called them "dinner plates." Her habit of forging or overreaching had caused her hind feet to often hit the back of her front feet, sometimes cutting the heel or leaving nicks on her legs. Bell boots over her hooves gave protection, and helped Fanny to think about where her feet were going.

Pam brought in Gene Wise, an experienced farrier she knew, from Rushville. During several visits, he gradually changed the size and shape of Fanny's hooves, which made her less awkward. Setting her hoof angle at fifty-three in front and fifty-six in back was the answer that stopped the forging. I had once complained about Fanny's rough trot; later I marveled how her long stride and smooth extended gait gave me a feeling of floating along. Some of that movement was improved muscle development and fitness, but much of it was the farrier's expertise.

Over a period of six months, from April through October, I watched Pam work with Fanny and perform her magic. For four months, Pam kept Fanny at her own barn. Fanny came back the same eager, headstrong mare that I loved, with a somewhat ornery nature and a stubborn streak and less than perfect conformation . . . but now she looked more beautiful than ever . . . cleaner and better groomed and her muscles were more developed. Now she was more willing, more supple, and less awkward. Her bull-headed nature was more controllable. She had learned to use her body more effectively, with better self-control. She had learned to calm down and listen, and let a human direct her where to go. You could safely touch her body almost anywhere, and her defiant attitude had mellowed. She was ready for the real partnership to begin.

CHAPTER 7

Taking Up the Reins

While Fanny was in Pam's barn, I rode her there as often as possible, sometimes with Pam's supervision. Fanny was turned out in a small paddock an hour each day, and Pam worked with her and fed her and charged me only for feed and supplies. I couldn't have found a better bargain anywhere!

But now Fanny was back home and I was learning to take charge on my own, trying to apply all that Pam had taught us. I learned, for instance, that a horse's actions and reactions depend largely on how I handle the horse. I tried to remember to ask myself, "What did I do to cause that?" Even the way I talked had an influence. I remember at first, I was so excited about my new adventure with Fanny that I often chattered continually in a high-pitched loud voice. Pam explained this could make Fanny nervous, but I would forget and chatter on. Sometimes Pam would quietly say, "Betsy, shut up," with an affectionate smile. As I learned to talk more quietly, it did help. *But I needed most to learn a calm, confident attitude.* I remembered Grandpa Moats telling me about someone who was always saying, "whoa . . . whoa now . . . whoa there" to his horse, and Grandpa chuckled that it only made the horse edgy. Better to say "Whoa!" once, firmly, he told me, and mean it (he raised his kids that way, too)!

"Know your horse," Pam taught me. "Know her temperament and level of ability and training." A horse's "bad" actions are more often caused by a lack of training, balance, or self-confidence than by meanness. A horse that won't let you pick up his feet, for example, may lack balance or trust, and punishment can only make it worse. Gentle patience in handling any horse, especially a young one, will gain better response in time than a constant badgering or punishment for every little error.

A handler's reaction must be immediate to be effective. I learned to watch for body language warning signs . . . ears flicked back suddenly, tail switching nervously, a hoof cocked not in rest mode, a head turned a certain way, wide eyes, or muscles suddenly tense. I tried to be ready to avoid the problem or to react to it immediately. While riding, for instance, I learned to be aware of Fanny's muscles suddenly getting more tense and to watch for that sharp forward snap of her ears. I knew these were signals of her intent to turn and run. I learned to be ready with leg pressure and rein control. I learned to use those aids before Fanny could whirl around. It was much easier to prevent a runaway than to stop her after she was going full speed!

My greatest problem with Fanny was her resistance to the bit. Considering that we had started with a severe bit too small for her mouth, and Mark and I both tried to slow her down by pulling hard on the reins, I couldn't blame Fanny for developing what Pam called "jaws of steel." Fanny was used to pulling back. Pam reminded me often to work toward a lighter touch on the reins, using pressure and release instead of a steady pull. Earlier in Fanny's training, Pam had used a snaffle bit with side reins on the lunge line to help teach Fanny a proper head set. Fanny couldn't hold a good head position for long, however, because her neck was too thick and her temperament too obstinate!

I tried several different bits. I even bought a special "spoon" bit that applied pressure on the sides of the mouth . . . a bit that I used for only a short time, and it may have helped some. Maybe. I tried a Billy Allen bit with long shanks and a three-piece snaffle mouthpiece. Fanny had a way of jerking her head sideways to take hold of the shank. Once she had that shank in her teeth, control was impossible.

I finally bought a Kimberwicke at the suggestion of a riding companion, about a year later. That was the solution. She couldn't take hold of anything and she learned to focus more on where she was going. She didn't slow down, but I had better control.

When we bought Fanny, she was not registered. Fortunately, her mother had been bred to a registered Appaloosa stallion named Apache-Lagrimas. Through his lineage, Fanny's great grandsires were Apache and Hawkeye, two foundation Appaloosas. As a five-year-old, she had one small white spot on each rump. Every year brought more white spots, gradually forming a handprint pattern, and more of the mottled coloring on her nose. I was able to register Fanny as an eight-year-old, under the hardship clause, because of her Appaloosa markings. Her registered name was "Fanny-Pepper," borrowing the

"Pepper" from "Pepper-Chinchilla," her great grandmother. We all felt the word pepper fit her temperament as well as her markings.

Fanny liked to run and she was always eager to go faster. I sometimes wondered what she would do if I didn't hold her back all the time. I was a cautious rider, always keeping a tight rein, afraid of a run away or a fall. I remember one particular afternoon, however, while riding on a neighbor's recently harvested soybean field, when Fanny's trot eased into a canter and it seemed quite enticing. I loosened the reins and touched her lightly with both heels. She responded immediately with an amazing burst of speed . . . she was faster than I had imagined! But instead of my usual fear, I felt a daring excitement! Her mane whipped in my face and I urged her on. "Show me what you've got," I whispered. For the moment, I eagerly thrilled at this new adventure!

Her gallop was free, open, and smooth with a generous lifting motion and my legs held on tightly. Enjoying this rare pleasure, I let her run the full length of the big field until we reached the other end. She didn't fight the bit this time when I tightened the reins, but slowed gradually as we turned. I remembered all the times Fanny had gotten loose and ran full speed all over our field before letting me catch her. This time, I had truly shared her joy in the freedom to run. *This time, our spirits had raced together.*

I remember another afternoon when I felt a restless need inside, but I had to leave for town in half an hour. I saddled Fanny without the usual grooming and I didn't hold her back. No prancing around, no warm up time . . . she trotted and cantered for a mile, then we turned and came back home just as fast. I usually would have walked the first half mile, warmed up with a trot before cantering and walked the last mile home. But that day, I had time only for a brief escape. As I removed Fanny's bridle, she bent her neck around, shoved my shoulder forcefully with her nose and nickered loudly. Was she asking why we didn't ride longer? Or was she saying, "That was fun!" Did she feel the special bond as much as I did? *Could she possibly know how much she meant to me?*

Pam has told me several times, "Fanny would have done anything for you. She tried so hard to do what you asked, even when she wasn't really able. She really loved you!" Did I truly believe that? Did I not realize how much? *Was it so difficult for me to feel loved . . . by a horse or by another person?* Fanny certainly gave me all that I asked of her with a loyal and eager heart. And her familiar whinny always greeted me as I neared the barn. Did I feel "unloved" merely because she had a mind of her own instead of being totally submissive?

In return for her service, I tried to take good care of her body and muscles as Pam had taught me. I used gallons of liniment on her legs and shoulders over the years, giving rubdowns after each hard workout. I loved the way she came alive after a liniment body wash. To help her dry off, I would lunge her a few minutes and she would break into a trot with a fresh burst of energy. Then I would hand graze her on the lush green front lawn for fifteen minutes as a special, relaxing treat for us both. While she ate grass, I often brushed her, talked to her, and combed her mane and tail. Seeing her feel good made me feel good, too. This was our time to bond, to just enjoy together that special feeling after a good ride, when all is well inside and out! I felt the partnership between us growing stronger. Fanny may have been Mark's horse for three years, and Pam tamed and trained her . . . *but Fanny was really mine!*

During those times, I also took time to really look at Fanny. Pam had taught me to watch her health by checking gum color and coat condition, by keeping daily watch on little things that could help prevent larger problems. I looked for cuts, bruises, skin problems, bumps . . . anything different or unexplained.

I looked at her eyes. Were they bright and alert or did she seem uninterested or tired? I learned to observe and sense things as I rode. I checked her moods . . . the way she walked, trotted, and cantered. I looked for uneven gaits and bobbing head. I learned to sense how she felt when fresh and the difference when she was tired. Pam told me that sore muscles, pain, or lameness could make her mouth feel hard instead of giving. It was most difficult to know whether she was hurting somewhere, or just being ornery and headstrong (her old self!).

Whenever I had a question or a problem, I called Pam for advice. She gave me a lot of her time, and I was deeply grateful for her help. Our relationship was valuable not only for the information she shared with me, but in the depth of our friendship. *I turned to Pam because I wanted to be like her . . . to be as good with a horse as she was.*

Training Fanny was a true investment of countless hours of time and energy from both of us. Few people want to go that far with any horse of small value. And Pam didn't even ride Fanny; Pam's satisfaction in this project came mainly from the verbal sharing of my joyful experiences. My obsession was encouraged by Pam's thorough attention to detail. Yet, I feel that Fanny's service was well worth our time. As a woman, I had a need to nurture and care for something that responded to me. *And Fanny did respond*. I felt great pleasure in my meticulous care of this energetic creature who worked with me as a willing partner. Fanny literally gave herself to me.

Fanny's response to my attention helped build my self-esteem, and her training gave me great satisfaction. I read many books and talked to many friends and teachers, but the actual step-by-step guidance from someone so experienced and willing was a rare and precious gift. On days when I felt discouraged and would have neglected my ride, Pam would somehow talk me into the saddle (She even yelled at me once!).

Looking back on that summer with Pam and Fanny, I remember it with great nostalgia. There were many times when Pam and I talked past midnight about horses, husbands, and life in general. Her encouragement kept me going. I wish I could remember all that she taught me, especially since I have had to learn it again and again (sometimes the well-known hard way).

Sometime that summer, in July I think, Pam loaned me her own new silver-trimmed saddle, and I entered Fanny in a Western Pleasure class. We had worked for weeks to get Fanny ready for this effort. I wanted to show her myself, just once!

That evening, before the horse show, I rode Fanny for more than an hour, trying to get her under control, to slow down. Pam rode her too that night, and reassured me that she was just being a mare, and it wasn't totally my lack of expertise. In the arena, Fanny was a great embarrassment when she practically ran away with me, right past the ringmaster (who worked with my husband). At that point, I understood Mark's frustration with Fanny more than ever before. *I decided that the show ring was definitely not Fanny's cup of tea . . . and it wasn't mine, either!*

CHAPTER 8

The Obsession of Competitive Riding

Since Fanny and I didn't do too well in the show ring, I wanted to find a sport that we could enjoy . . . something in which she might excel.

Somewhere in my borrowed magazines, I had read an article about distance riding. The writer's account of his first ride made it come alive. I thrilled with the author as he raced over the countryside from the exciting start to the emotional finish. Fanny was competitive and she was fast. But would she be able to handle a rugged trail and a fast pace for several hours? Would I?

During Mark's 4-H meetings, I had met a woman experienced in such rides. Jan Worthington, I later learned, was one of the top distance riders in the Midwest. She encouraged me to try competitive riding and offered to trailer Fanny to our first ride. I even took Fanny to her place and rode with her a few times.

A Competitive Trail Ride is a timed event over varied terrain, usually twenty-five or thirty miles of marked trail. The given time may vary from four to five hours, depending on weather, distance, and difficulty of the trail. The winner is the horse and rider who finish within the designated time period with the highest points (based on the horse's condition). Scores are determined from examination by qualified veterinarians and their assistants, with low pulse and respiration readings the key to winning. Points are taken off for lameness, fatigue, dehydration, a sore back, or bad manners. In some areas, riders are also judged for their horsemanship.

Distance rides in the Midwest are held almost every weekend all summer, with both competitive and endurance rides the same weekend. I never tried an endurance ride, which is more like a fifty or hundred-mile race. An endurance winner is basically the rider who comes in first with a sound horse. Thirty-mile limited distance endurance rides have been added since I stopped participating in such rides. I wish I could have tried one of those!

A good distance horse needs a long stride and the stamina to maintain a good trot for long periods. Fanny already had a good stride and she had the "heart" to go the distance. I needed to work on her endurance. Getting Fanny in condition for a competitive ride would require working out almost every day.

Pam suggested we start a serious conditioning program: Walk a few minutes, then trot a few minutes, gradually increasing the trotting time over the next two months. There was a nearby ride the first weekend in October and my goal was to have Fanny ready by then. Fanny was eight now and in peak condition with high energy, getting plenty of good feed and hay. She was kept in a stall except for an hour turnout in the paddock, and I rode an hour or more about four days a week.

In late August, I moved into an apartment not far from Pam's barn. I just couldn't handle the situation at home any longer. My husband and I were having problems every day and he didn't want to see a counselor with me. I didn't want to be around him, so with mutual agreement, I moved out. I would hurry to my apartment from work each night, change clothes, and ride until dark, then go back to my apartment for supper.

By mid-September, I was lunging Fanny at least fifteen minutes before I dared to get on her. She would buck, run, whirl around, and switch directions without warning. I let her work off the excess energy before I saddled her, and it made a good "warm-up."

There was a hilly forty-acre pasture around Pam's barn that was great for building muscle. I would trot Fanny about forty-five minutes all over that pasture, and maybe let her walk a minute after an uphill climb if she seemed to need it. We cooled down by walking a half hour before I unsaddled her and put her back in her stall.

She handled that exercise program well, and she seemed quite ready for the October 1st ride. At the last minute, circumstances kept us from getting to that ride, a loss I mourned the rest of my life! Fanny was in peak condition then, more so than anytime later. We missed her best opportunity, I believe, to place on a ride.

I resolved to resume Fanny's conditioning the following spring, but Pam was busy with other pursuits by then, and Fanny and I were on our own. Although I called Pam when I had problems, Fanny's conditioning suffered noticeably with the lack of Pam's coaching and discipline.

I hoped to have Fanny ready for a June ride. Three days before the event, however, I tried to make up for lost time, pushed too hard and Fanny showed signs of lameness. I called Jan, heartbroken to miss another ride. She offered me the use of an Arab who had not been ridden for three weeks, after doing a hundred miler. She assured me that he would not buck, and although I was not usually eager to ride strange horses, I gladly accepted.

My first look at the horse was the day before the ride, as she loaded him into the trailer. Next to Fanny, he looked skinny. He was a very tall gray that challenged my ability during the ride to mount in a hurry while other horses were already on the go!

Jan told me to stay off his back, to keep him trotting and not canter him, and I would have to push him a little toward the end of the ride. I rode the full twenty-five miles as a novice, on the hilliest and rockiest terrain I'd ever seen. It was beautiful! *When the results were called, with ten riders in the novice division, I was handed the trophy!* I know the horse helped me win; being one of Jan's Arabs, he was experienced at distance riding. Being an Appaloosa owner, however, I was quiet about riding an Arab. As I went up to receive the trophy and the winning ribbon, my tears glistened and Jan laughingly exclaimed, "She's hooked!"

My introduction to the sport of distance riding led to a great obsession. Although I was never able to do more than two or three rides a year because of family responsibilities and financial limitations, my mind constantly held onto this all-consuming desire to get Fanny in better condition so she might win! *Just once, I wanted Fanny and me to place on a Competitive Ride . . . even if it was Fifth Place!*

Later that year, Fanny and I did compete on our first competitive ride. I started the ride with Jan and several other riders, but her pace was faster than Fanny and I had been practicing. It was a difficult ride with long steep hills. Two-thirds of the way, Fanny's respiration was elevated, and she was hot and overexcited. I had let her rest for several days before the ride, and she had gained weight, which now added to her problems.

I wanted to stay with Jan, who knew the best pace to win. She assured me that we would slow down toward the end of the ride, but I was afraid to push Fanny too hard, not sure yet what her limits were. I told Jan to go on without us. We would walk awhile, even if we didn't finish. *It was not an easy decision.*

Fanny was upset to be left behind, but she quieted down soon after the other horses were out of sight. Her long stride at the walk covered ground easily, even though she was tired. We continued on alone, following a marked trail we'd never ridden before. *I will never forget the special awareness of the bond between Fanny and me that day, as we shared the experience of this new challenge.*

Sometime later, Fanny lifted her head and whinnied. I nudged her and she willingly broke into a trot. A little further, a marker read "two miles" to the finish line and I checked my watch: twenty minutes of ride time left. New excitement brought tears to my eyes. *I suddenly realized that Fanny and I could still finish our first competitive ride on our own!* That moment of my life was a precious treasure.

I kept Fanny moving at an easy trot along the winding wooded path. Just ahead, Jan's group was walking the last mile. We fell in behind them and crossed the finish line with one minute to spare. If I had stayed with Jan, Fanny's score might have been better with more time to recover . . . or she might have had serious problems. I didn't want to take the chance. She gave me an excellent ride, and I was thrilled to finish on time. We didn't place, but I felt a great satisfaction at completing the ride without endangering her health. And everyone who completes a ride gets a prize, I learned!

Walking was difficult for several days; my legs weren't used to riding twenty-five miles in four hours! I was too happy to complain much. I showed Pam my completion prize . . . a beautiful belt buckle . . . and shared every detail of the ride. She grinned proudly when I pointed out Fanny's high score for extra good manners during the vet's examination. We talked that evening for hours, sharing my joy in this accomplishment.

Fanny and I finished our first three competitive rides, not placing on any of them. After every ride, I would go home determined to follow a more consistent conditioning schedule, but something always interfered. If I was tired, I would tell myself I'd surely ride tomorrow. *I lacked the drive just when I needed it most!* My family was always finding more important things for me to do, and I allowed it. If I put my demands ahead of theirs, I felt guilty! *Did I have the right to stand up for my own goals?*

Fanny was pulled from the next two rides at halftime. On the first ride, I had shared a trip all the way to Wisconsin in a large 4-horse rig. The weather was perfect and the ride terrain was easy. The group I rode with moved steadily at a good pace. When we reached the two-mile marker toward the end of the ride's first half, I wanted to walk. Fanny was doing great, and I wanted low pulse and respiration readings for a higher score at the vet check. The others wanted to keep trotting to make better time, so I stayed with the group, walking only the last half-mile.

All four of us were pulled from the ride for high respiration! Fanny's reading was forty-eight, and forty or less was required to continue the ride. I hopefully asked for a ten-minute re-check. Her second reading of forty-four was still too high . . . and my ride was over.

Why didn't I trust my own judgment as I had on Fanny's first ride? Why did I stay with the group when I knew what might happen? I left the group on the first ride only because of my concern for Fanny's welfare. This time, however, I was more concerned with Fanny's reaction to being left behind than with winning!

The next ride taught me a different lesson, more difficult than most. The trail that day was mostly downhill, quite steep, and very muddy after a heavy rain . . . and we moved along at a strong trot. Twice during the first fifteen miles I thought I felt an uneven gait, but Fanny was pulling hard at the reins so I let her go on. When I dismounted at halftime to lead her to the checkpoint, I noticed a pronounced head bobbing. She had pulled a deep shoulder muscle, I later discovered, which took six months to heal.

I remember standing alone on the hillside after the halftime period, holding Fanny and watching the other riders disappear in groups into the wooded area beyond the pasture checkpoint. The vet crew had finished their exams and had headed back to the base camp to send a trailer back for us. Fanny whinnied and looked around anxiously, and I couldn't hold back the tears.

Fanny had given me her best. She kept pace with the other horses in spite of her pain, and I didn't realize she had a real problem. I learned that Fanny would often keep going when she was hurting, which made it difficult for me to distinguish between that and her natural competitive spirit. But I felt terrible about her injury.

When I started out in competitive riding, I was using a long-shanked snaffle bit, hoping for more control; but Fanny would turn her head to one side and fight to take hold of the shank with her teeth! When she did get hold of the shank, she was impossible to stop! On one ride where the trail became a narrow path at the top of a steep hillside, Fanny was concentrating so hard on getting hold of that shank that I was afraid she might lose her footing! I imagined us rolling down that steep hillside any moment!

Another time, we rode the trail with a group the evening before a competitive ride and Fanny ran away with me three times in an hour, breaking away and exciting the other horses. That didn't please the other riders, including Jan, and she suggested I get a Kimberwicke bit, which has no shank. I bought one as soon as I got home from that ride and I used it from then on. *I finally had the control I needed!*

In some ways, Fanny was a really good distance horse. Even on our first ride, she handled this new challenge with good sense and obedience. She loved to run, however, and her headstrong nature and competitive spirit showed in her desire to stay in the lead! She would slow down only if she was alone and tired. If a horse caught up with us and passed, she found energy to go faster, trying to get ahead. *She wanted to win as much as I did!* There were times when I tried to hold her back while other riders continued, and it was difficult and even scary! Staying with a group rather than riding alone helped her to stay calmer and took less of my energy.

I remember another ride, when after supper I foolishly put a hibachi with hot charcoal inside my camper top for extra warmth. I almost didn't live through that experience! I should have read the warning on the bag that charcoal fumes are poisonous! My husband happened to go on that ride with me and got me out into fresh air after I passed out! The fumes didn't get to him as soon as they did to me. It was one of many times that I felt God protected me. The next morning, I needed help to get up into the saddle and I had little control of Fanny during the ride. She literally ran away with me the first five or six miles, and she was dripping sweat at the first vet check. I thought sure her respiration would be too high to continue (and I even hoped we were done) . . . but she passed! We finished the ride . . . which may have helped clear my lungs faster than normal, according to the doctor I visited after I got home.

Fanny had a long stride, whether at the walk or trot and she felt solid under me. I didn't worry about her tripping and falling. She navigated steep hills and ditches quite easily. One time, I came over a hill to find two young riders trying to cross a wooden bridge, their horses refusing to attempt this new footing. Fanny hardly hesitated, and the girls' horses followed. We crossed knee-deep streams when she'd been unwilling at home to walk through a mud puddle! We trotted over strange new roads and open fields, up steep rocky hills and narrow wooded paths, past large farm machinery and pastures with cows (just like the ones that used to spook her).

Fanny's only problem was her high respiration readings that hurt our score. She was an excitable big mare with a tendency toward shallow, fast breathing. I would have built up her stamina and increased her breathing capacity with lots of cantering, but whenever I tried that, she seemed to go slightly lame. I concentrated on lots of trotting.

She had a thrilling extended trot! I remember coming down a hillside, riding alone, when I saw Jan's group almost half a mile ahead on a level field. *I asked Fanny for more, and I felt those strong legs reaching out beneath me and her body twisting and stretching with the effort.* I stood in the stirrups and held onto the horn of my saddle. We caught up with Jan and the others as they reached the creek, even though they had been cantering across the field. *At times like that, I knew Fanny could win.*

In 1981, Fanny was eleven years old. We started three competitive rides that year, finishing only one . . . our last event together. I remember walking for long periods on that last ride because Fanny's respiration wasn't coming down.

It wasn't the usual hot August weather, and I kept worrying . . . why wasn't she doing better? *I knew, however, that I wasn't able to get her fit enough with my schedule and my lack of discipline.* I realized I was taking a chance at another injury . . . and for what? I decided that day that

I would not put her through this stress again, even as the tears ran freely down my cheeks. I could no longer see a purpose in my efforts. I knew it was best to quit, for Fanny's sake . . . but it was so difficult to give up this dream that had consumed me for three years. She was going through all this . . . for me! I was the one who had the obsession! I was the one wanting to win . . . even though Fanny's competitive spirit had been my inspiration!

Two events in 1981 were emotionally overwhelming. First, my dad passed away in March, and settling his estate required many long trips to Iowa that summer. I wonder what my life since then would have been . . . if I had moved into Dad's vacant home. It was mine now and the thought of starting over on my own was very enticing . . . but I didn't have the courage to actually do it! I wanted to write and learn more about riding . . . but I was afraid I couldn't support myself.

Meanwhile, I was taking a course in real estate because my husband wanted me to get my license. I didn't want to sell real estate, but because of his "encouragement," I'd already paid the fee and started the course. I came home from the second session to learn of Dad's death.

Then one day a neighbor stopped to talk while I was riding and during our conversation, he made an innocent remark. "If you loved your husband," he said with a grin, "as much as you love that horse, he'd be one happy man!"

I wish I hadn't reacted to that remark as I did. After the neighbor went back to his fieldwork, I got off and unsaddled Fanny and put her away. After that, I worked in the garden and I cleaned house and I rode only when I couldn't stand it any longer. Fanny and I lost the magic of our partnership. I lost my greatest joy. Without regular exercise, Fanny lost fitness and condition and was sometimes stiff and lame. Every partnership involves two beings. *Who was I punishing?*

Years later, I realized how much I had given up. Just when I needed Fanny most, I turned away because a neighbor's words prodded my inner guilt. Perhaps the physical exercise and the feel of an energetic horse's companionship would have helped with my healing. I learned another great truth. *Any relationship weakens with distance, whether horse and rider, husband and wife, or a spiritual relationship with God Himself.*

I had left Wes in August of 1978, went back six months later, mostly from guilt and fear of being alone, and felt trapped. I quit my job in 1980, after Dad's accident while cutting down a tree, because I wanted to spend some time with him while I still could. Wes didn't approve of my not working, however; he said he needed help paying the bills. He had this attitude that I wasn't doing my part unless I was earning money!

I had become resolved to accept a lonely life with a family that didn't seem to understand, doing what everyone else thought I should do. At least I had a place to keep Fanny. *Did I stay in an unhappy situation just so I could afford to enjoy this horse and rider experience?* No one seemed to understand, at least not the neighbor! Pam may have been the only one who really did understand.

Fanny was the innocent victim. Her intermittent "lameness" led me to ask an instructor to ride her. She believed Fanny had a chronic stiffness that would improve if she were ridden consistently. I was too easily discouraged, however, to be consistent. It was too much work, and I was too tired, and too depressed. I wondered if her stiffness was a partial consequence of that pulled muscle during the competitive ride.

Although I still enjoyed riding Fanny now and then, I never again took the time to nurture and maintain our partnership the way I had before. Many years later, I realized that although I had neglected this special partnership, Fanny was still always there for me!

With Dad gone, I felt my "family" was gone, even though Mother was still alive and I talked to her now and then. I was used to running to others for help and comfort, and I still ran to Pam quite often. I had been too dependent on Dad's encouragement, because Wes was emotionally distant and always busy. I felt totally alone at times.

My greatest strength came from my Heavenly Father, who gave me a comforting sense of His Presence throughout the entire ordeal of Dad's passing and the funeral itself. There was an amazing impression of being at peace even though the loss was great. Little details just seemed to work out right. I couldn't help but feel a deep thankfulness for all Dad meant to me and for all that God was doing. He had even led Dad and Mother to get reacquainted and find a sort of "closure" before Dad died.

God had given me much . . . a wonderful father, a good horse, an unusual friend, and many good experiences in life. *Perhaps it was God's mercy, making up for some of the unhappy times.* I appreciated His involvement in my life, more and more.

CHAPTER 9

Memories that Stir Imagination

For the next two years, I stayed close to home, riding less and less. I had leaned on Dad so much that now I felt alone and afraid and I found myself withdrawing inside. I tried a sales job—a huge mistake! Every refusal sent me home to nurse my wounds. I didn't deal well with rejection.

Just before Dad died, Wes and I had talked about divorce again, our second attempt, and Dad had invited me to come live with him. Now Dad had left me a home, fully paid for, in a small town where I knew people. With Dad gone, however, I just couldn't find the strength to make the move and strike out on my own. I wasn't sure I could support myself or deal with the many issues of living alone. It was, perhaps, another opportunity lost . . . but I told myself I was doing the right thing.

In 1983, Wes was transferred to an office in St. Louis, Missouri. For a year, I stayed on the farm with our youngest son who was attending a local college, and Wes lived in an apartment closer to his work. I often spent weekends house-hunting with Wes in the St. Louis area.

In March of 1984, during one of those week-ends, Fanny injured herself and was chronically lame the rest of her life. Running through the open barn door one evening at feeding time, her right front foot landed on the pole at the doorway. My vet took x-rays and said she had a mild case of navicular. Another vet later looked at the same x-rays and said, "I see no sign of navicular!"

Hoping the injury was muscular, I rubbed lots of liniment on her leg and shoulder to bring down the heat. Several months later, she seemed sound and I rode her moderately. Then she ran hard in the pasture one day, jumped a ditch, and was lame again. Fanny was fourteen that year, too young to be a cripple.

I often wish I'd had the emotional strength to take Fanny and move to Dad's old home when I had the chance. Fanny might not have been in-jured and perhaps we would have placed on one of those rides after all! Instead of going into real

estate, which my husband pressured me into, perhaps I could have followed my own chosen field
of interest. Hindsight is never there when you
need it! On the other hand, it could have been a
disaster! You never know until you try.

For seven years, I tried arthritis supplements,
different vitamins, liniments, massage, and special therapy, looking for a "cure." Five years later,
I found that half a Bute tablet daily was the easi-
est way to keep Fanny comfortable. At that time,
I was giving basic walk and trot riding lessons to
three or four young pupils and the exercise
seemed to be good for her.

Realistically, I knew Fanny would never start
another competitive ride. And yet, I secretly
hoped for a miracle. I struggled vainly for seven
years, pushing her to do what she could not do,
discouraged at her inability to canter on her right
lead without going lame. I missed the excitement
and the wonderful sense of working together that
Fanny and I had previously enjoyed. I missed
her strength and energy that made me feel truly
alive. Perhaps that same attitude, always hoping for more, made me stay in the marriage.

Six rides in three years with no winning ribbons was nothing to brag about. But my memories of those rides with Fanny were precious.

I remember cool fall mornings . . . as forty or
fifty riders made their way to the starting point

through the early haze of dawn to be suddenly engulfed in a stampede of energy.

I remember lying in my cozy sleeping bag at night, staring up at the twinkling stars through the camper top window, planning tomorrow's ride strategy and savoring every sound. Throughout the night, as I woke from time to time from a restless snooze, I could hear the low rustling of blanketed horses munching hay or rattling a water bucket. Sounds of pawing . . . a whinny . . . and answering whinnies. *Who could sleep with the excitement of a ride beginning in the early morning?*

One night . . . actually, it was 3 A.M., a whip-poorwill perched above the camp and echoed its shrill endless repetitive cry. From inside one of the campers I heard a muffled "Shut up!" I couldn't help but chuckle, immediately hearing a soft rippling sound like many chuckles from here and there all over the campground.

Another night, I curled up in my sleeping bag on the front seat of my pickup truck (a storm had destroyed our camper top). With the window open a crack to let in fresh air and mosquitoes, I woke to hear the sound of a horse walking along the gravel road outside. I peeked out, disturbed to see a blanketed horse being led back and forth along the path, apparently having a problem with colic. The next day, our ride was delayed a bit while the vets worked to save the horse from dehydration. With an IV, and extra blankets loaned by various competitors, the horse pulled through.

I remember the cheers from those on hand late the next day, as this horse was well enough to load into his trailer for the ride home. Here was another reason I enjoyed competitive riding: The riders were usually more willing to help each other when help was needed, than those who competed in the horse shows I'd seen!

Fanny was not my only distance horse, but she was my original motivation. She could have done better, if I'd managed my own life differently to help her win. In some ways, I felt I had failed her. *Fanny couldn't reach her full potential without discipline, but my own life needed more consistent discipline before I could help her.* Perhaps my greatest regret is not going further with Fanny and the competitive rides while I had the chance. I wish I'd given it my all in spite of everything else. Not because Fanny needed to win . . . but because I needed to!

Through my distance riding experiences, I learned not only about horses and Fanny and winning, but I learned a lot about myself and some of it was difficult to absorb. I saw how important it was to ride my own ride, to follow my convictions. *Even though I didn't always do it.* I learned the value of persistence. I came to realize that each small step toward a goal really did have meaning. If I wanted to win, I had to be sure of my goals and keep working toward them. I couldn't get discouraged and quit, which I often did. I had to learn to stand firm against my own doubts and negative comments from others. I wish I could say I learned those lessons well! They applied not only to competitive riding, but also to life itself!

Like Fanny, I could be headstrong at times, yet anxious. I held back, afraid to follow God's leading over difficult paths. I worried about my problems instead of asking God for guidance, listening for His direction, and trusting Him to work through me. Without focusing on Him, I was easily distracted. Overwhelmed by inner turmoil, I was afraid to make decisions.

I often followed others who seemed stronger and ended up in a different direction than I'd planned, wishing I could have gone my own way. Even so, I wanted someone else to take charge, take the responsibility, and help me. I was too much a child, needing permission to do what I wanted! *I didn't dare to live my own life!* But mostly, I was afraid to grow up . . . afraid to stand up for myself!

Over the years, I have started twelve competitive rides with 5 different horses, but I never felt the obsession to win with any other horse as much as I did with Fanny. I loved her headstrong, eager spirit that took me beyond my fears, even though she was nervous and impatient. *Her energy made me feel alive and strong.*

Fanny and I earned four completion awards. I also have the novice trophy from my ride on the borrowed Arab, and a Fifth Place ribbon earned by an Arabian mare I owned later. But the ribbons and trophies weren't as important to me as the experiences that Fanny and I shared. She was the "wind beneath my wings," in a very real sense.

The thought of a competitive ride still makes my heart race with memories of special excitement. I am grateful for those experiences that enriched my life, and the many lessons I learned, and I feel I have been allowed more joy with a horse than most.

Sometimes, I think I should try once more to condition a horse for a twenty-five-mile ride, just to see if I could do it. And then, I consider my age and energy level and I remind myself that a wiser man than me once said, "For everything there is a season . . ."

Letting go of an old dream can open life to new opportunities and different challenges! I still need to work on applying those things I learned and integrate them into my life. And I can still apply to any new challenge the lessons I learned from my previous competitive experiences. There are definitely many ways to enjoy a horse!

CHAPTER 10

Parallel Trails

The spiritual message of this book began to surface and develop after an incident one evening back in the mid-70s. It was Fanny's feeding time, and she was especially impatient! I was scooping feed out of the barrel, and Fanny was running in circles in her stall with her ears back. Now and then, she would stop to paw the floor or bite the stall door. I was getting a big kick out of her expressive nature, and as I stirred a handful of wet bran into her feed, I enjoyed scolding her a bit.

"Fanny, behave yourself! I know you're hungry. I'm getting your supper and you'll just have to wait a few minutes till it's ready. Be patient!"

Suddenly, it was as though someone tapped me on the shoulder and whispered in my ear. *"It's the same with you and Me. I know what you need and I will provide. Be patient."* I was totally startled! But I immediately knew that those silent words had come from God. He had spoken to me in thoughts from His Spirit!

Alone in the barn that night, I felt a fearful and special reverence. I quietly gave Fanny her supper and I pondered those silent words. Yes, I was impatient at times, just like Fanny. But . . . was there something definite I needed to be more patient about?

Sometime later, on a warm, sunny day, I decided to go out for a long ride alone to explore new territory. I saddled Fanny, packed a snack and a hoof pick, and rode off down a country road we had not seen before. I watched ahead carefully for potential problems, since Fanny was always spooky when ridden alone in new areas. Her ears were forward and her step was springy and hesitant.

In the distance, maybe a quarter of a mile away, a white cat ran across the road. Fanny stopped immediately, flicked her ears and tucked her head. Her whole body tensed, and I knew she was getting ready to turn and run. I gave her a gentle kick to urge her forward, keeping a tight grip on the reins.

"Fanny, you foolish mare! That cat isn't going to hurt you. Now behave yourself." I tried to relax and make my voice confident and reassuring. "You don't understand, but I know it's all right. That white cat is a long way off and it's running the other way. You don't know about cats, but I do. Come on now, Fanny, you've got to learn to trust me!"

Suddenly, I felt another gentle nudging and these silent words, *"You too! You are so anxious about things you don't understand. But I know about them. Trust Me!"*

I was awestruck! I knew I wasn't imagining these silent words that entered my thoughts. God wasn't just scolding me . . . He was encouraging me to have more faith. He had given a promise, "I will provide," and a command, "Trust Me!" I felt like Moses before the burning bush . . . but there was nothing to see, only words to remember. As I continued to work with Fanny, I often sensed God's influence, and I began to see many similarities between the relationships of horse and rider, and God and man.

Meditating on this concept one day, I asked myself, *Why do I want Fanny's trust?* The answer: *So she will be safely manageable in threatening situations.* Her safety as well as mine is at stake. Without trusting my control, she will react in her own fearful ways, which could be dangerous! If I am not in control, then my horse is. I must find ways to build a strong trust so she will depend on my guidance.

Fanny often spooked at things. She ran away with me when we met a truck pulling a mobile home, bucked me off when I tried to carry a lunge whip, and reared when a motorcycle passed us . . . all because of her fears! Some riders seek to control by force, but I think that only increases the fear. If I want my horse to go where I ask in spite of fear, trust must be created before the need for it occurs. I wanted Fanny's trust and respect for my control to overcome her fear of unknown things. At least she was able to cross a wide knee-deep river during a competitive ride. One day we met a train almost head-on a mile from home. When I wouldn't let her turn and run, she backed up across a ditch into a tall cornfield, knocking down about twelve rows backward, then stood shaking until the train sounds faded!

God knows my trust in Him could be my only real strength when facing my own fears of the unknown. That trust has already been tested, and I have known God's comforting Presence when I needed it most, at the loss of my father and when I almost lost a son, just to mention two situations. I felt God there beside me, enclosing me in His protective love, revealing His compassionate control over difficult circum- stances.

I still struggle with a weak and inconsistent faith. I struggle with His control just as Fanny struggled with mine. I make choices without seek- ing His will . . . and I struggle with the results. Sometimes I can see God's love and power at work in spite of my doubts and stubborn will. I often wish I could trust God more completely! *I need a faith that is stronger than my fear, a faith based on the power of His Word and His authority.*

I've seen that a good relationship between horse and rider does not always begin with a purchase. *It begins when the rider learns to take charge in a way that the horse accepts.* Sometimes there is a struggle before the horse chooses to yield. If the rider asks too much too soon, the horse may rebel. The sensitive rider learns to work patiently and kindly toward gain- ing the horse's cooperation (just as God works with us!). Once that step is reached, the horse is often obedient from then on. It is the accep- tance of a confident authority that begins the true working relationship.

In church, I was taught that a genuine spiri- tual relationship with God had a definite begin- ning based on surrender and commitment. I remember the moment when I experienced that beginning in my own life. It came when I accepted God's authority, believing in Him and His Word and specifically yielding to His Sovereign will.

I remember the struggle within my soul as His Holy Spirit worked to convince my stubborn heart. For many years, I had felt Him urging me toward a commitment of my total self. I didn't want to give up my freedom, however. I was afraid of what He would ask me to do. I wanted to be a Christian, but I was trying to do it in my own way. After I saw the death of my beloved Grandpa Moats in 1966, I began to think more seriously about my own mortality and what my life on this earth was meant to be.

I thought I was a Christian because I was raised by Christian parents, believed in God, prayed, and went to church. I was confirmed in the Methodist Church as a teenager. I took communion. I was told to do my best and God would understand. Was that really all there was to it? How could I be sure?

Something deep inside me believed there was something more! I read my Bible enough to know that Christ had told Nicodemus, "You must be born again" in John 3:7. *I wanted to know what that meant.* Even though I had been baptized as a baby, I wanted to be immersed as an adult, just like the disciples. I wanted my Christian experience to be genuine and meaningful . . . even as I held back on a total commitment.

I believed that Jesus Christ was the Son of God and that He died on the cross. His sacrifice paid for the sins of the whole world. I knew I could choose, however, to live my life as I pleased or to surrender totally to His control. Was there any middle ground? Could I live my life my own way . . . and still make it to Heaven? If I lived my life as I wished, what would I miss that God wanted for me?

Then one day, a minister and his wife came to call and invited us to attend a new church that was getting started in the area. We were impressed by their sincerity and their message. Hearing a different viewpoint on salvation and what it meant, I became uneasy during his sermons at the possibility that I wasn't a real Christian after all!

I asked questions and studied my Bible. I prayed for God to forgive my sin. I wanted this assurance of salvation that the people talked about. I had prayed once before with another minister who told me that I was saved. But I hadn't felt anything and there had been no difference in my life. I wanted a definite knowing! I wanted my belief to make a difference! Now, I had come to the place where nothing else mattered as much as my assurance. I wanted to believe 1 John 5:13: "I write these things to you who believe in the name of the Son of God so that you may know that you have eternal life."

Then one morning . . . I suddenly understood. All the questions and answers, the Bible study, and the sermons finally made sense and I felt God telling me that He had already taken care of it. *Christ's death on the cross had paid for MY salvation and I need only accept His Word in faith and allow God to take over and work in my life.* I realized that this was the only way I'd ever have peace with myself and with God. My decision was made, and joy and peace overwhelmed me. I felt free of past guilt and anxiety . . . free to make a new beginning!

The Bible says that His Spirit witnesses to our spirit that we are His, and that's just the way it was. I suddenly knew with great certainty that it was true. I remember the exuberant words in my heart, "I am His . . . and He is mine!" After years of avoiding and postponing this moment of surrender, it had come; and I realized the commitment of that surrender was my new birth! And it was very, very real!

I had tried to be a Christian by doing the right things and trying to live the Christian life . . . by my own human effort. Now, I gave the reins to

God. By submitting to His Sovereign authority and allowing His Holy Spirit to direct my life, I found His power at work. *It was no longer my efforts alone doing it . . . it was the indwelling of His Spirit working within me and through me.* Being a Christian was not something I tried to make happen; it was happening because He lived within me and I allowed *Him* to do it.

A horse does not do intricate dressage movements without a rider who gives him the cues. And he still would not do them until he has been trained to understand those cues and has learned to accept and obey the rider's authority.

We cannot be genuine Christians without Christ actually living within. That is the first step . . . to be sure we have invited Christ Himself to penetrate our lives! Only then can we begin to learn to understand His great love and guidance and to accept His authority and obey it. In the Bible, 1 John 5: 11–12 says, "And this is the testimony: God has given us eternal life, and this life is in his Son. He who has the Son has life; he who does not have the Son of God does not have life."

Sometimes, we have learned to rely so much on ourselves and our own goals and abilities that it is very difficult to let God take charge. With age, we get more set in our ways, more cautious, more hardened against taking risks. We learn to control our circumstances as much as possible in order to protect ourselves . . . but God asks us to give final control into His hands. He wants our loving obedience, but He does not force us to do His will. His love gives us the freedom to choose. Sometimes it takes a critical life experience to cause us to turn to God for His help.

My relationship with Jesus Christ began with a step of faith. It continues based on faith. *The real struggle of life is not to be good enough, to obey a set of rules or to be perfect, but to simply yield my will to His . . . again and again, day by day, moment by moment, as I am able to do so.* In the process, He continues to work with me, teaching me how to sense His guidance and understand more fully what He expects from me (just as a trainer works with his horse!). I know that many people may not agree with these thoughts, but my own heart feels certain they are true. Even though I have not reached the place I want to be, I know that only God can get me there.

Once we know the assurance of eternal life, our true purpose in this life is simply to glorify Him in whatever circumstances we find ourselves. We no longer need to struggle to get to Heaven! *He is able to take us from wherever*

118

we are . . . no matter how seemingly helpless or unholy a place that may be . . . to a position of eternal glory with Him. We must learn, however, to submit our will to His and cooperate with His leadership. If we place ourselves into His hands, allowing His guidance—even His discipline—He becomes our protector and counselor. The "secret" of living a Christian life is to let Christ live it in and through us. *His Spirit will help us develop the ultimate harmonious working relationship, God and man in partnership.*

God is a "Gentle Master" who calls to us . . .

Come to me, all you who are weary and burdened, and I will give you rest. Take my yoke upon you and learn from me, for I am gentle and humble in heart, and you will find rest for your souls. For my yoke is easy and my burden is light. (Matthew 11:28–30)

CHAPTER 11

Follow a Plan

*I*didn't buy Fanny to turn her out to pasture and feed her apples over the fence. I wanted to actually do something with her.

I had a plan for Fanny. I wanted to train her myself, to feel pride in watching her become the great horse I knew she could be. I had to admit I didn't know how to do it on my own, but then Pam came along . . . and she shared my desire to develop Fanny's potential. I wanted to enjoy riding Fanny and take good care of her. She was an exciting companion. I wanted her to win a competitive trail ride, because I wanted others to know how special she was and that we could accomplish great things together.

Fanny and I were a lot alike. Without the struggle of dealing with her problems and seeing her need for discipline, perhaps I would not have understood as clearly the need for discipline in my own life. Without that discipline, neither Fanny nor I could accomplish the goal.

Through the concept of this parallel relationship with God, I began to see His point of view in a way that I would never have seen otherwise. Just as I had a plan for Fanny, I believe God has a plan for my life, too. He does not force His ways upon me, however. In His wisdom and love, He gives me the freedom to live as I choose. *But if God has shaped a specific plan for my life, how can I find its true fulfillment without His guidance?*

My plan for Fanny depended both upon my skill as a rider/trainer and upon her abilities, temperament, and willingness to cooperate. God's plan for me has the same components, but God's skill is unquestionable. God knows my potential and He knows exactly how to develop it. My part is to learn to depend on Him . . . to allow Him to give guidance within our intimate relationship and to develop my willingness to work with Him toward the fulfillment of His plan.

The woman and her Arab in the Coliseum had learned to work together in an effective partnership. I am still learning about how to achieve such a relationship and each horse is different. I am also attempting to apply what I learn in a parallel manner to my relationship with God.

I remembered how Fanny used to be. She never stood still and I did well to avoid a smashed toe while working with her. She was easily distracted and excited. While ridden, she was always pulling on the reins, recklessly eager to go faster. And she spooked at anything that moved or made noise.

When I was teaching her to sidepass, she tried so hard to figure out what I wanted that she got frustrated and upset. It took a lot of patience to help her simply quiet down and "listen" to my cues. Meanwhile, she tired herself out with efforts that got her nowhere! She was struggling to do things that she didn't need to do!

I considered this "image" of Fanny one day and I realized . . . it was also a picture of myself. Frustrated by a problem, I tried to figure things out by myself before simply turning to God. I worried and talked to everyone, looking for answers. I wanted to fix the situation immediately. It took a lot of God's patience, I think, to help me stop and listen to Him. Yes, Fanny and I were much alike. We struggled to find our own way to do things, when we just needed to patiently stop and wait, and listen to the direction of the one in charge.

"Lord," I prayed, "Help me calm down and focus on letting You take control!" He reminded me to "be still, and know that I am God!" (Psalm 46:10)

For some reason, it's difficult for me to calmly let God be in charge when things seem really scary! But as I allow Him to be Master in a specific situation, He brings about the results that fit His plan. When I fall, He helps me up. When I resist His way to go my own, I often experience a time of struggle and frustration until I put it all back in His hands again. That struggle may last moments . . . or years!

A horse does not understand the rider's goals. And we do not fully understand what God is doing. *Trust must go beyond understanding.* Without the willing submission or cooperation of a trusting partner to the responsible leadership of the other, there is no true partnership . . . there is only conflict.

God's Word continually tells me to trust and obey Him. *Since He knows and understands all things that are "unknown" to me, it would make sense to obey the One in charge!* We teach our horses to obey us, because we know about most of the spooky things that our horses must face out on the trail. God knows much more than any of us, no matter how brave and knowledge-able we are. We just need to learn to spend more time with Him, seeking to learn who He is and what He can do!

The more I put into my relationship with Fanny, I realized, the more she meant to me. The effort, the sacrifice, the struggles and the worries, all blended into a deeper affection that strengthened our bond. *Those struggles, with Fanny helped me understand how God was try-ing to work in my own life.* And this realization helped me accept my own struggles, both physi-cal and spiritual, as a precious growth process toward greater spiritual maturity as well as the opportunity for a closer bond with God.

One of my greatest joys was to see Fanny's response to my training efforts. I was pleased as she became more obedient and controllable. I could do so much more with her. We could en-joy our times together even more. Perhaps as I became more obedient, God could enjoy doing more with me, too.

Did God feel a similar pleasure in my per-sonal development and spiritual growth? Did He actually enjoy our times of fellowship, when I went to Him in prayer and studied His Word . . . when I just sat at His feet and worshipped in His Presence and waited for Him to teach me what I needed? Was He sad when I let other things crowd out my private time with Him? Did He know beforehand the problems I would have because I went my own way? Was He angry when I did things I knew I shouldn't do? Or deeply grieved? Somehow, considering my feelings for Fanny as a more tangible comparison, I could understand His regard for me differently now.

I remembered when Fanny got hurt because of her foolish actions. I was angry with her for being headstrong, but I understood that she was just being Fanny. I loved her anyway, and I took care of her hurts the best I could.

God understands me more fully than I understood Fanny. He must feel grief when I cause pain for myself or others and He knows I will have to suffer the consequences of my decisions. He has helped me through many serious problems, and I have grown stronger . . . more than if He had removed those problems! *But in fact, His love has already borne the worst consequence of my sin for me!* The nail prints in His hands were for my salvation. He took my punishment, to give me eternal life!

I have always believed in God, just as I have always loved horses. But I didn't truly know horses until I owned one. *And I didn't really know God until I actually experienced His "ownership" of my life*. Becoming responsible for Fanny taught me something about God's task of being responsible for *me*! Fanny had a mind of her own and she sometimes did things I didn't like. But I never quit trying to bring out her best, because I really loved that mare! As strong as my feelings were for Fanny, I realize that God's unconditional, unfailing love for me is immeasurably and supernaturally stronger.

As a human being, I often feel inadequate, but I know it is Christ in me that makes me adequate. It is His plan for me that gives real fulfillment and satisfaction and success in life, when my own plans often fail. *It is His power at work that transforms my life into more than I could ever accomplish on my own*. Being human, I often make mistakes. I hope someday to do better and I will . . . as I learn to depend more fully on His Holy Spirit. Trusting Him more completely and obediently allowing His Spirit to be in charge, I know I will find His plan unfolding and His wisdom revealed.

And I marvel and wonder at His greatness.

"For I know the plans I have for you," declares the Lord, "plans to prosper you and not to harm you, plans to give you hope and a future. Then you will call upon me and come and pray to me, and I will listen to you. You

will seek me and find me when you seek me
with all your heart." (Jeremiah 29:11–13)

CHAPTER 12

Hope of Glory

The young woman riding a gray Arab in the empty Coliseum was still a vivid image in my mind. I remembered my impression of the graceful "oneness" of horse and rider moving together. Unlike magnificent performances in the show ring, with resplendent costumes and the pressure of competition, this had been an honest, quiet revealing of a basic working relationship.

I could still see the subtle, disciplined movement of that woman as she posted, and the collected stride and submissive energy of her horse. With the memory of that image compelling me, I was determined to become a more skillful rider in the arena.

Back then, I didn't yet own an English saddle. I had a sense of partnership with Fanny from the competitive rides and I was a better rider after all those miles, but English riding was different. I wish I could have started Fanny with dressage training; she had the ability before she was injured, but it was too late now to ask that much of her. She still had plenty of energy and spunk, if I could limit my demands to her present capability. It never occurred to me to want a different horse.

I wanted a specific training program to get me started, but I needed discipline to consistently follow that program . . . and I knew that such discipline had been lacking as I conditioned Fanny for the competitive rides. As always, I wanted someone to help me, to make me do it! I wish that I could have learned more completely the lesson of taking charge of my own life! Something within my brain still needed work!

Pam had previously told me it was important to work with Fanny every day. If I was not consistent, she said, training would take longer and I would get discouraged with the results. How right she was. Although my riding goals were different now, the same principles still applied. Pam had cautioned not to let others ride my horse. Even though basic cues are the same, different riders can confuse the horse and slow the learning process. If I wanted a special harmony with Fanny, I should be the only one riding her.

This philosophy had always caused a conflict with my husband, who said horses weren't any good unless other people could ride too. He often invited people to come and ride, and I worried about someone getting hurt or hindering my training efforts.

I realize now that from his viewpoint a horse was just an animal for people to enjoy and he simply wanted to share what we had. My point of view, however, was based on a desire for the ideal working relationship between horse and rider that I had seen in the Coliseum. How could I expect a husband to understand my need for that kind of relationship with a horse? Did I myself understand? I had enough to do, he felt, taking care of a home and family and helping earn money to pay our bills. Not that those tasks weren't important or that they weren't enough to occupy my time . . . but that lifestyle alone only magnified my inner need! If my marriage had involved a closer, more intimate loving relationship . . . would I have needed Fanny as much?

I had seen a connection between horse and rider that for some reason motivated and drew me. I wanted to know that connection with Fanny. For some reason I couldn't explain, it was extremely important. Just as I had earlier felt an obsession to win a competitive ride . . . now I wanted to learn to ride English.

Something else was emerging from my experiences with Fanny, however, beyond the principles of horse training and my own personal growth. I was impressed by the circumstances that led us to buy only Fanny when I really wanted Honey. Then, as I tried to take Fanny to a professional trainer, one obstacle after another stopped me. Then I met Pam. I became aware that God Himself seemed to be directing this scenario and that all these things were not coincidences. I believe with all my heart that I was meant to have Fanny, and Pam was meant to teach Fanny and me . . . and God was somehow behind it all! *I am convinced that God deals personally with each one of us, using our experiences and interests to get our attention*. What better way to reach someone who is interested in horses . . . than to use horse related experiences?

Looking back at my struggles with Fanny, I can see many times when God used a situation to teach me something of great value in my life. Although I am certainly aware that not everyone will agree with my viewpoint, I share our story in the humble hope that each reader may find God's touch somewhere along the way.

Sometimes, if we view a scene from a different perspective with a mind that seeks eternal truth, we can see beyond the visible objects and movement of daily events. We can gain insight on how or why . . . or find meanings not usually comprehended. Though I saw physically only a horse and rider circling an empty arena, I saw more than the product of years of horse and rider working together with a consequential harmony and mutual purpose. *When I looked at that scene through memory shaped by spiritual perception, I saw a demonstration of spiritual truth.*

As I remembered that woman riding her Arab in the empty Coliseum, I also saw God and man, learning to work together toward spiritual partnership. As I thought about the attentive obedience of that trained horse and what a skilled rider could accomplish with a horse, I began to sense a demonstration of Scripture. The phrase, "Christ in you, the hope of glory," in Colossians 1:27, had always puzzled and intrigued me. Now, I could actually visualize it being acted out through this horse and rider!

This may be difficult to follow, but with imagination plus logic, the illustration should emerge. *A rider expresses himself through the movement of a willing, obedient horse as they work to-gether in harmonious partnership.* The rider gives subtle cues and the horse obeys. This level of communication may take years of effort and training before the horse reaches that degree of willing obedience. The end result can be seen in a magnificent performance when horse and rider move together as one!

God also expresses His life in and through people who are indwelt by His Spirit, as they learn to trust Him and obey His Word. That, too, may take years of struggle and experience before human submission is refined to that degree. As Christ lives in us, through His Spirit, we learn to allow His guidance day by day through many subtle cues, including prayer, Bible study, circumstances and counseling.

We can learn, as a horse learns, to follow a Master's guidance, to be obedient to His will. *And the result is a glorious partnership between God and man . . . working together toward an eternal goal!* I wanted with all my heart to find that kind of deeper, stronger working partnership with my own Heavenly Master!

A serious trainer guides his horse to higher levels of performance, striving for the glory of winning. The training process requires much time and patience, concentration, and focus on a specific goal. Jesus Christ lovingly guides each believer, through the power of His Spirit, toward greater maturity and inner strength in His Word, confirming the hope of eternal glory with God the Father. His patience is great as He teaches His ways and helps us understand what He wants from us.

If I could learn to be as submissive as that horse, I wondered, *what could God accomplish in my life? How could He use me to influence the lives of others?*

I believe God purposely led me to the point of asking that question. He helped me look at submission from a different viewpoint than I had ever known. I had resisted total surrender to God, afraid of what He would ask me to do. Even though I believed in God's authority, I was still struggling with my own independent spirit. Now I was seeing the glorious result of a yielded spirit, even that of a horse, and I wanted a higher level of performance in my own life . . . a level I knew I could not attain on my own! *God had taken me past the struggle, to see a glimpse of its achievement.*

I wanted to experience God's leadership in my life. I wanted to be obedient to that guidance, even though I struggled with my own stubborn will! Why couldn't I learn that kind of partnership with God? I was praying for help yet resisting the very help I was asking for! At first, I told myself that this goal would take time and patience to find fulfillment. *Yet, I really knew that experiencing God's leadership was merely a matter of yielding to it.* It is that simple.

Harmony with God requires submission and commitment to His will. Living with the reality of human nature is different than visualizing the ideal, however, and I realized sadly that I was as far from the ideal as Fanny was! I hesitated at total surrender, partly from fear of losing my identity. *I wanted to live my own life . . . to enjoy my chosen pleasures.*

I saw how Pam worked to enhance Fanny's natural ability without breaking her spirit. A trainer looks for a horse with unique personality and flair . . . a horse that is a "good mover." Then the trainer works to bring that talent under control . . . not to lose its identity . . . but to reveal its brilliance! I was reminded of 2 Corinthians 5:17, "Therefore, if anyone is in Christ, he is a new creation; the old has gone, the new has come!"

Submission to God's leadership *is* a new start. It helps me live life more abundantly as Jesus Christ promised in John 10:10. I once believed that total submission meant giving up my freedom. To gain the harmony of "oneness" with God, I must depend on Him and seek His guidance on a daily basis. I had known this kind of relationship briefly, though it seemed to disappear when my independent attitude persisted. Sometimes I actually felt God working in my life, but only when I allowed His guidance with a willing heart.

Recently, I have realized another aspect of submission. Even as we have a choice . . . to live for self or live for God . . . we also have a motive for that choice. Do I choose to obey God for the reward of a "brilliant" performance in life . . . or out of fear of hell . . . or because I can acknowledge with my whole being that He is my worthy Lord?

Total submission allows His total protection and care. We don't realize what we are giving up by holding back. We must overcome our fears, doubts, and independent natures to live fully within the intimate, ultimate fellowship with our loving Father. In our connection with Him, there is healing of fear and loneliness, and there is empowerment beyond our weakness. Total surrender to our Creator leads to maximum blessing here on Earth and in eternal glory, maximum victory in our everyday lives, maximum usefulness and greater access to the power of His Holy Spirit.

To recognize His Sovereignty means to also recognize my own humble place in His Kingdom. Does a horse ever have an "ulterior" motive of accomplishing fame as a jumper or Grand Prix horse? Doesn't a horse submit to its rider first and foremost because he acknowledges the rider's authority?

Perhaps the willing cooperation we find in our horses is meant to be an example for us.

CHAPTER 13

Meeting Sally Swift

I first heard of Sally Swift while riding Dude with a new friend. Charlotte quickly observed that I was not following Miss Swift's basic principles. Fanny's only offspring, Dude was an unpredictable youngster and I didn't feel secure while riding him. Charlotte noticed I was staring intently at Dude's ears. Actually, I was watching for an early warning of his next decision to run away with me.

Dude's first ride away from home, as a four-year-old, had ended with me on the ground. I had been riding along a narrow path between a tall cornfield and a fenced half-acre pig lot, when he spooked at the pigs and bolted. I turned him back, but he bolted again in another direction. I turned him back again, but then he gave a mighty leap into the cornfield. I had knotted the reins together at the ends, and catching over the horn of my saddle they both snapped about a foot from the bit. I went off over Dude's rump. I'm sure the cornstalks broke my fall, but I distinctly remember a feeling like many gentle hands lowering me to the ground and I was not hurt. Dude stopped at the edge of the cornfield, wide-eyed and prancing, apparently too scared to know where to go. I had no trouble catching him.

After that incident, I was afraid whenever I rode him. The day I rode with Charlotte, Dude was acting unusually tense and jittery and I was on the verge of panic. My new friend took the time to briefly explain Miss Swift's basic principles and how they could help me.

The first principle, Charlotte explained, is simply to breathe freely and regularly. The second is to look up at the horizon with "soft eyes" that see all of one's surroundings, instead of "hard eyes" that concentrate on one place. Looking up made me sit down into the saddle and relax. *A moment later, Dude was walking calmly along with his head down where it belonged.* I couldn't believe the immediate change. It was too easy!

Charlotte rode with me about an hour that day, continually reinforcing this new technique. Each time Dude became jittery, she reminded me to breathe deeply and to look up . . . and every time, Dude immediately relaxed! It was too good to be true! Charlotte had taught me only two of Miss Swift's four principles and I had found a new enjoyment of this young horse. That day's experience convinced me that my own nervous tension was causing Dude's jittery movements, and "soft eyes" and breathing could control the situation.

I wanted to know more about Miss Swift and her four basics. So when she visited a local saddle club for a clinic, I signed up to audit a class.

As I watched her work with each group, I admired her ability to see the needs of both horse and rider, and to work with any level of skill. I was impressed with her serene ability to keep control in various riding situations. She concentrated on the rider's posture and body control as a means of good communication and influence. Correct posture and balance of the rider allowed the horse to do his best, she said. I left the clinic with a greater appreciation of good horsemanship. I was determined to apply these newfound principles to my own riding experience.

I learned that Miss Swift began riding to strengthen her back, having problems with curvature of the spine when she was quite young. She mentioned studying with Jean Gibson of London, but much of her teaching is based on the Alexander technique of muscle relaxation. Studying under Peter Payne, she worked several years with his "body energy awareness" clinics. She felt his techniques greatly improved her posture and inner balance and she went on to apply them to the skill of riding.

She taught four basic principles. *The first basic is the "hard eyes . . . soft eyes" approach.* Hard eyes concentrate on one object (such as the horse's ears), shutting out an awareness of much of one's surroundings. The body tends to stiffen, and the horse may become fearful, reacting negatively as Dude did. But when the rider looks up and out with soft eyes that take in a larger perspective (including the horse's head), the body relaxes. *The horse relaxes, because a rider's soft body is more comfortable than a rider's stiff body.* The ability to see with soft eyes must be learned and practiced, but it results in greater awareness of the horse, of one's own body, and everything around, through all of one's senses.

Your eyes can see more than you think, according to Miss Swift, if you allow them to. You shouldn't be *looking* at your horse, however, you should be *feeling* him beneath you. I remember her words during the clinic, "If you glaze your eyes or look just at your horse's ears, you will miss half the feeling through your seat." You must train yourself to widen your awareness of what you can feel and learn that you can actually see much more with soft eyes!

Breathing is the second principle. A tense person tends to breathe shallowly or to stop breathing momentarily. The horse feels this tension as discomfort, and may interpret it as fear. "You must allow the body to breathe fully, from the diaphragm," according to Miss Swift. "Breathe out during a moment of stress or during a transition. Regular breathing helps to establish positive communication with your horse."

The third basic, "centering," requires the rider to imagine a spot deep within the lower torso as the center of energy, control, and balance, and to work from that center. Miss Swift was constantly reminding her students to "center . . . and grow." A tree does not push itself or stretch, she says, "it just grows." She wants the body to remain soft and relaxed, free and open, yet controlled by energy radiating from the center. This involves both concentration and imagination. Using this basic principle, my own posture and depth in the saddle has improved. Working from my "center" of control helps me tuck in my tummy and "lift" my upper body without tension and stiffness.

The fourth basic, "building blocks," depends on the first three working together and actually deals with balance. At this point in Miss Swift's presentation, she reaches for a small wooden box and asks, "Have you all met Herman?" She uses a small replica of a human skeleton to illustrate how the rider's body affects the horse.

She positions Herman with an imaginary line through ears, neck, shoulder, hips and ankle. "Your seat may change . . . the length of your stirrups may change," she cautions, "but you must always ride with your center over your feet. Get over your horse's center of gravity for good balance!"

Miss Swift describes her techniques in vivid language. She encourages her students to feel pulsations or ripples from the horse's motion and to receive that motion and not resist. She says the minute you stop feeling the ripples or pulsations of the horse's back, you begin to offer resistance. *And if you are not receiving that motion, if you are resisting in any way, your body stiffens and the horse cannot give you his best.* The rider must stay soft (relaxed) and supple, receiving the motion of the horse and allowing it to move his/her own body as they work together.

Miss Swift recommended applying her basic principles to all of life, even beyond the realm of horsemanship. I can truthfully say these principles have greatly contributed to my own insight and understanding when applied to the spiritual dimension.

For example, using the principle of "soft eyes," I can learn to perceive a wider view of life with greater wisdom and understanding. Instead of concentrating on a problem with so-called "hard eyes," I need to see it in proper perspective as a small part of life's enormous horizon. Instead of looking only at "self," I need to look with compassion upon a larger world of people.

I realized one day that I viewed life with the same attitude with which I rode. I saw life with hard eyes. I looked for things to go wrong. Because of my fearful attitude, I rode hesitantly with a tense body and mind, not breathing deeply. I missed the joy of living the present moment and I missed the peace of trusting in God's provision. Looking up and out toward God's eternal values and His great resources, I can relax and become aware of greater opportunities and dimensions of living. *I can dare to ride and live with more courage and purpose.*

Miss Swift's second basic parallels a concept of spiritual breathing I had learned long ago as the essence of communication with God. The idea is to regularly "inhale" His Word through Bible study and meditation on Scripture, and to "exhale" by confessing all known sin through prayer. I keep a vital relationship with God not by trying harder to be good, but by humbly revealing my needs continually to His mercy and power and allowing His Spirit to work in me.

During times of temptation and stress in my life, this practice has given strength and peace and a sense of precious communion with God. When I neglect to breathe spiritually, the results have been anxiety, tension, and a loss of purpose, as well as a feeling of distance from His Presence.

I believe that spiritual breathing is as essential for one's spiritual life as physical breathing is necessary for physical life. Spiritual breathing should have great depth and freedom, without the hindrances of guilt, fear, doubt, or unbelief. We need to spend time alone with God on a regular basis, every day, to deal honestly with each issue we face.

The term "centering" has different meanings in various philosophies. In Phillips' translation of Romans, chapter one, Paul states "The Gospel is centered in God's Son." *The Gospel is the message of God's grace and power, shown by the death, burial and resurrection of His only Son, Jesus Christ.* God has continually urged me to center my life on Jesus and not on myself, money, material things, man's traditions or on other people. Since God is the source of all things, it makes sense to center my life on His Word. Centered on anything else, my life soon becomes unbalanced.

Miss Swift's reminders to "center . . . and grow" were frequent. In my own life, too, I need this frequent reminder, at the beginning of each day, after an upsetting incident, or whenever I sense a change in direction. I need to stop and check my spiritual posture and center again on the basics of Christ and His purpose for my life, growing spiritually from the experiences He allows in my life.

Growing takes place in its own unique way, not from a struggle, but from response to light and food and the freedom to be. *Within the freedom of God's grace, strengthened by the food of God's Word and led by the light of His Spirit, my spiritual growth should be natural and healthy.* Sometimes I try to make it happen and get impatient when it doesn't. Sometimes I neglect to take time for adequate nourishment.

I need to learn to find my inner balance and depth of power from the Christ that lives within me. Centering on Him, I learn to deal with life from a positive belief in His love and direction. Without a strong inner conviction, I am easily distracted, discouraged, or confused by the many directions life offers.

Just as Miss Swift's fourth basic depends on the first three working together, I have seen how my spiritual balance depends on a strong foundation of God's Word. I must build on the true doctrine of Jesus Christ, not on man's traditions. If I follow a leader, church, or movement that is not following Christ's teachings in proper balance, I lose my own stability.

If I pray and study, yet neglect to apply what I have learned, my growth is hindered. Sometimes I have experienced God's teachings over and over again just because I failed to apply them before. God's Word should make a change in my life. *Each basic principle of horsemanship or spiritual truth comes alive only as it is put into use . . . as it is applied and learned and becomes part of the individual's way of living.* It takes consistent effort, a plan of action, and many reminders.

The best part is knowing God is in control and He will not give up on me. His loving mercy is everlasting. His patience is never ending. His commitment to keep me as His own is faithful.

Of course I still worry at times. But I am learning to appreciate the gift of life itself, and finding joy in living life more fully. Realizing how much God has given me, I am thankful for each special moment and each blessing. I find myself seeing more of life's possibilities, and a greater horizon. *I am learning to apply to all of life what I have learned from the horse and rider experience, just as Miss Swift suggested.*

CHAPTER 14

The Victory of Obedience

*A*uditing one clinic with Miss Swift wasn't enough for me. I dreamed of actually riding someday in a clinic, although I believed that "someday" would be a long way off. The announcement came much sooner than expected that Miss Swift would be giving a riding clinic in my area . . . and I was challenged to make my dream a reality!

It was Stella Cotton, a friend who knew of my dream, who suggested I sign up for the clinic. I didn't have the seventy-five dollar fee, and didn't feel ready to ride English, but Stella kept encouraging me until I put my name on the list. She even loaned me her own Passier saddle (the very saddle I later purchased). I'm glad she gave me that push. Miss Swift soon began scheduling her clinics for instructors only, rather than individual riders, and I believe that clinic would have been my only chance!

One week before the scheduled clinic, I realized I had another obligation. This was the weekend we had agreed to host several members of a traveling singing group giving a Sunday morning concert in our church. So here I was, committed to a riding clinic on Saturday and Sunday . . . with guests coming! My husband offered to play host and cook the meals for four young men so I could attend the clinic. For once, I was glad he enjoyed cooking.

The clinic included a Friday evening talk by Miss Swift, during which she explained her four basic principles and how they applied to riding. On Saturday and Sunday, I actually rode in a group lesson for almost two hours each day.

I have absolutely no memory of Saturday's class. This was a year or two after Fanny's shoulder injury, and her abilities were barely adequate for a two hour session. But I do remember Sunday! It was cold, and I was late getting Fanny loaded. My rear view mirror had broken off the driver's side of my truck, and some of the trailer lights weren't working. I felt guilty for not being home to be a proper hostess and for not attending church. I wouldn't even hear the group sing. Everything seemed to be going wrong. *I remember praying, "Lord, please help me to find a victory today! I'm so tired of frustrations and defeats . . . tired of feeling like a failure!"*

Fanny was stiff from Saturday's class, and it affected her skills during Sunday's group lesson. I was embarrassed at our performance, but Miss Swift was patient and very understanding. She encouraged me and gave me some things to work on but didn't push me to do more than Fanny could handle.

I was tired and discouraged, but thankful for this special opportunity. The clinic was almost over when I noticed a big, fat turkey waddling toward the open barn door.

Oh God, please make that turkey go away! I prayed silently. But God and the turkey had other plans. The turkey was still there in the doorway when Miss Swift asked us all to exit for the next group.

I had carefully kept Fanny out of sight of this turkey for two days, even leading her around behind a barn or horse trailer to avoid a confrontation. I knew she would explode at the sight of this strange little monster. I rode over to Miss Swift and explained, "Fanny doesn't like turkeys. I won't be able to get her out the door."

Miss Swift didn't seem one bit as concerned as I was! She calmly said to go ahead and try it. As I directed Fanny toward the door, my predictable mare took one look at the turkey, tensed up and scooted backward about twenty feet like she'd seen a ghost. "Sit . . . sit . . . sit!" Miss Swift insisted. I sat. "Eyes up, seat down. Sit!" I did what Miss Swift said as though I was hypnotized. "Breathe!" I did. *And Fanny walked out that door, right past the turkey!*

"Good, Betsy, good!" Miss Swift called after me. I could hardly believe what had just happened. I felt the surge of emotion in my stomach and chest and the tears flooding my eyes. I rode Fanny past the red barns to the outdoor arena and walked her around the well-worn track. We both needed to relax before heading home. Fanny was prancing, and my legs were shaking. Tears were tickling my cheeks. Walking past a turkey may have been a simple task for others, but it had been a major incident for Fanny and me!

In the past, I had stayed on as she jumped sideways, bolted and ran, or backed off like a crab, but I had never been able to make her walk past a scary object as she had just done. I admired Miss Swift's ability to control the situation as she did. In a sense, she passed her confidence on to me through her commands and I received it and obeyed. I remembered a scene from the clinic I'd audited years earlier. Miss Swift had told a young instructor, "You've got to believe it will work, and then it will. Your horse will know it . . . when you do!"

I remembered too, my prayer that morning. I had asked God for a victory and He had given me one.

For this moment, I felt strong, triumphant, and in control! As soon as Fanny and I had calmed down, I dismounted and led her back toward my trailer. God wasn't through with me yet, apparently, for there beside my trailer the turkey stood waiting. I decided it was time to take advantage of my unusually confident mental condition while it lasted. I led Fanny toward the turkey, watching her carefully. She moved a few steps, then stopped, her ears sharply forward. I waited, then slowly led her another step, then another. We were about ten feet from the turkey when I saw her muscles tighten for a sudden leap backward. And that's what I was waiting for.

"No!" was all I said. But my tone was firm and strong, and for some reason deep inside me, I actually believed she would obey. *And she did!* She stood still, eyes still on the turkey, but I think there was surprise in her expression.

Something was different, and this time she did as she was told.

I led Fanny another step forward. Then another. She was only a few feet from the turkey, head down, but moving slowly forward with a gentle blowing sound now and then. I was praying that the turkey would hold still, when I sensed the old fearfulness creeping back into my mind. I quickly took a deep breath, stood up straight and thanked God for my new confidence. Another step and Fanny's muscles tightened again.

"No!" My tone was firm as before, and she stood without backing off. I patted her neck and told her what a brave girl she was. She reached out with her nose, slowly, hesitantly, almost touching the turkey. I asked no more of her. Tears were filling my eyes again and my heart was pounding with the wonder of this experience.

Fanny snorted softly and flicked her ears. Then she reached down and grabbed a bite of grass. I laughed out loud . . . the pressure was relieved and I realized that the turkey had lost her total attention. I patted and rubbed her neck and let her eat. The turkey stood nearby for almost ten minutes before wandering away. I wanted to tell someone what had just happened, but everyone was busy either riding in the clinic or loading up to go home. *Only God knew what He and Miss Swift had done for me that day.*

Home again, in old surroundings, my new confidence faded back into old habits, except for one incident some time later. It was a warm summer afternoon, and I was preparing to give several horses a bath in the shower stall. The stall door was a wide wooden gate that swung open when not latched. After finishing one horse, I laid the hose over the open gate. The nozzle end was turned only partially off, on purpose, allowing the water to drip into a bucket, just to lower the pressure.

Bringing Fanny from her stall, I led her by the halter . . . which isn't a safe method, I know, but we were in an enclosed arena. Just as we approached the shower stall, the water pressure apparently increased suddenly from the pump cycle. The end of the hose actually rose up in the air, waving a sprinkle of water toward us as we neared the shower stall door.

In that instant, I consciously decided not to look at the hose. I focused totally on going forward toward the crossties within the shower stall, holding Fanny by the halter, talking quietly. She was between me and the hose, so I was definitely not in a good position. The hose continued to wave and sputter, then fell off the gate, writhing in the dust like a snake. *Even so, Fanny followed me into the stall without hesitation.*

Usually, Fanny would have stopped, backed off, and refused to walk on past the hose. Or she might have pulled loose from me and ran off. But this time, I had controlled the focus of my thoughts away from the fearful object and Fanny stayed with me.

Did my mental focus really have such power over my horse? Fanny had walked past a scary turkey because I followed Miss Swift's calm authority to relax my riding posture . . . to sit, breathe, and look up . . . instead of conveying fear through my usual tenseness. Fanny had stood still in a fearful situation just because of a confident authority in my voice. She had walked past the snaky hose because I focused on going forward instead of on my fear. *I realized that Fanny's obedience certainly was influenced by my attitude and the focus and control of my mind, voice, and body.*

It was awesome to realize the effect of this power of confidence and authority when dealing with a horse. I could see the great advantage of a confident trainer with a firm kind voice over a nervous or fearful person with a shrill uncertain voice. I believe a horse must trust his owner and feel safe in that owner's care. A horse needs to respect the rider's authority and feel secure with it. *And the human must feel secure in his own authority!*

I see an important parallel here. Our victory as Christians is based upon obedience to God . . . just as my victory with Fanny came from my obedience to Miss Swift's instructions. I listened to her guidance and followed it, and it worked! As Christians, we need to follow God's guidance obediently to have victory.

When we take time daily to read the Bible, study what it means, and apply it to our lives, we will find that it does work! When we know God's Word in our hearts, His Spirit can use those words as encouragement and guidance. His guidance, therefore, is partly based upon our knowledge and use of His Word.

When riding Dude, different instructors told me to sit quietly and keep my hands steady. I was pumping my body, trying to encourage Dude to go, instead of trusting him to do the work. I was actually interfering with his balance. But I never felt confident that he would do as I asked! I learned I had to give stronger, more definite riding aids and gain his respect so he would listen and obey. I had to take charge firmly, without being unkind. I had to learn better control and use of my own body.

Friends also commented that I worked too hard at trying to be perfect, both spiritually and personally. *I worried too much about my human weakness, which made it difficult to focus on God's power.* I had to make a conscious decision to focus on trusting God and obediently allowing Him to do the work within me.

It is miraculous to me that God can and does work through imperfect human beings to do His perfect will. Miss Swift's words, as I obeyed them, gave me control of Fanny as I could not have had on my own. It was Miss Swift who was in control; I only did as she instructed. Through my obedience to her words, I operated out of her knowledge and ability. She actually took charge and I trusted her direction.

Ephesians 6:10 confirms this principle. The writer says to "be strong in the Lord and in his mighty power."

It is *His* power that works through man's weakness to overcome the obstacles that we confront. It is *God's sovereign authority*, through Christ, and through His Spirit that helps us during life's struggles and temptations. We have power because of God's Spirit living within us. *That power is released through our human efforts when we choose to allow His Spirit to lead us.*

If I am trying to do everything from my own human resources, I am not using His power, even though it might be available. If I had ignored Miss Swift's words and ridden my usual way, Fanny probably wouldn't have obeyed. To use His power, I need to learn to be aware of His guidance, allow His direction and be obedient to it.

Scripture says that God wants us to live in victory, not failure. Confidence is not always easy to produce within ourselves. But we can depend on His authority and power, on His strength and wisdom. It is real and it is available; we don't have to just think positive or try to make it happen. *We only need to acknowledge the reality of His greatness and trust the unconditional state of His love and mercy toward us.*

A horse may have difficulty understanding what his rider wants. In time, as the rider patiently and consistently reinforces each cue, the horse learns what it means. He learns to trust and obey this rider. As humans, we should have a greater capacity of understanding and learning ability than our horses. We can learn to be aware of God's Presence and to identify His guidance. *We can learn to obey that guidance, to be like a channel of His power and His love for others as it works within and through us.* We can learn to trust His love and wisdom.

God has given mankind the freedom of choice. A horse may be willful and headstrong, just like man, but a human trainer does not usually offer as much freedom as he is given by his Heavenly Master. Some trainers use force, others use patient understanding. The difference, perhaps, is based on compassion and love. Only love can give another being the freedom to be an individual. Love will draw, while force will push away. You may force behavior, but you cannot force the desire to please, or the willingness to cooperate. You cannot force that special bond with your horse. It is a gift from the animal.

Just as I listened when Miss Swift told me to sit, breathe, look up, and balance my seat . . . and I did and it worked . . . in just that way, God's Spirit whispers quietly into our spirits . . . to seek His guidance, focus on Him, and trust His Word for instruction and correction. As we listen and obey, He works it out in our lives and through our actions to minister to others who also need His love. We become part of His Kingdom and His eternal purpose, sharing His glory.

I know life's victory is more than completion awards and trophies. It's keeping a positive belief in Jesus Christ and trusting in His unlimited resources in spite of fears and problems. It's a strong and abiding faith in His Word even when

162

things don't go my way. Victory does not always come from a struggle to do better; it can come merely by yielding to God's Sovereign leadership. Our victory is not in our individuality and independence . . . but in our individual dependence upon Him and our obedience to His will. *Victory is in our focus on God's direction rather than forcing our own way.*

> *Dear Lord, whisper Your words of guidance and encouragement into my listening ears. Take me to the place where I can more easily hear those silent whispers of Your Spirit. Help me overcome my fears and selfish ways. Help me to have the courage to follow You with an eager, willing spirit wherever You lead. Let me hear and obey so that I will experience victory over the obstacles before me!*

CHAPTER 15

Finding My Balance

Wes never understood why I spent so much time with a horse. He said I was neglecting him and the boys. They seemed to believe I was meant only to take care of them. "That's what women are for," my husband said jokingly when I complained about having to clean up a mess he'd left. *Why couldn't he see the terrible need inside me?*

Wes and I were both raised to believe that a man was the head of the family and woman was created to be man's "helpmate." I wasn't happy with the way he exploited that belief. I felt a desperate hunger for a sense of closeness . . . of "oneness" in our marriage. I needed his comforting arms more than his working orders! Since I felt more partnership with a horse than with my husband, I was told that my priorities were out of balance. I didn't yet have the sense to see it might be his priorities as well!

During Miss Swift's riding clinic, she taught an exercise to help a rider find balance in the saddle (and she said to apply her teachings to all of life!). With feet out of the stirrups and keeping the whole length of the body very straight, the rider leans slightly forward just until the leg and tummy muscles catch for support. Again, keeping the body straight, the rider leans back until those muscles tighten. Leaning forward then back, the rider seeks a quicker awareness of that moment of muscle support, until the upright position of true balance is found. The rider should sense the difference between *holding* the body in an upright position and *feeling true balance* in the saddle (*was I holding myself in a family position that was out of balance?*).

The first time I did this balance exercise on a horse, I was amazed to feel a profound sense of sudden physical relief at my point of balance. It was an epiphany of peace and a moment of mental awareness of incredible emotional freedom! I wanted to sit there in this euphoric state as long as possible, but horses don't stand still for long.

A horse moves, and the rider tightens up as his balance is threatened. A good rider learns to go with the horse's movement. The rider strives for *relaxed balance* and good riding posture as the horse walks, trots, canters, or turns in various patterns. Some riders have good natural balance; others may need hours in the saddle or lessons with various balance exercises to achieve the ability to move gracefully with the horse.

How could I find the inner poise to move in greater harmony with the conflicts of daily life . . . and with my family? Did I need more counseling? I'd had a lot already! How could I apply this exercise in physical balance to the personal realm?

I habitually ran to others for help with decisions. I often felt pulled in different directions, leaning one way toward one person's ideas, then another direction toward someone else's opinion. I read books. I asked counselors for advice. I certainly did not have secure emotional balance and was afraid to stand firm on anything!

I considered the words "relaxed balance" and tried to compare that phrase to my personality. I was definitely not a relaxed, serene person! I wanted to be a "good" rider and a "good" Christian who relied on God's guidance. But I was too easily influenced by other voices. How could I learn to make my own decisions with the ability that God had already given me . . . and be more sure of myself?

Since a spiritual perspective is the basis of my personal well being, I knew I needed spiritual answers. I wanted to be sure of my spiritual "position" in Christ. Just as Miss Swift taught us to seek physical balance on a quiet horse, I realized I would find spiritual peace more clearly during life's quiet moments.

My favorite place for that mission is a park or woods, where I go alone to sit awhile. I remember what God has done in my life. I read Scripture and pray. Applying Miss Swift's suggestion to "center . . . and grow," I try to center on Jesus Christ and who He is . . . on His unlimited resources as the Son of God. I imagine myself "growing" inwardly up and out, to realign my spiritual posture with His will for my life.

I sometimes find the peace I seek only when I collapse at His feet and let His Presence hold me. Sooner or later, I must get up and go on, back into the reality of making decisions and dealing with conflicts. It is the taking of His Presence with me that gives me balance even as life's situations change. Isaiah 26:3–4 assures me, "You will keep in perfect peace him whose mind is steadfast, because he trusts in you.

Trust in the Lord forever, for the Lord, the Lord, is the Rock eternal."

I greatly admire Miss Swift, and others, who appear confident in the midst of pressure (as in a riding clinic dealing with several riders at different training levels). Uncertain and fearful of making a mistake, I would rather let others take charge. A few times I have let someone else take control then wished I had done things my own way . . . but I still tend to feel uncertain! I do recognize the need to make my own decisions and find more confidence in what God can help me accomplish.

As a young adult, I got rattled easily. Recently, when I missed a turn-off, I tried to quickly back a horse trailer into a driveway to turn back onto a busy highway. Traffic was light, and I was able to handle it. I am learning to stay calm and focus on the task at hand. As I practice this ability, I have learned that it is easier to handle such things.

I remember the feeling of incredible victory riding Fanny past the turkey as Miss Swift told me to sit, breathe, and look up. *That experience became a symbol of my need to listen to God's guidance in times of stress, and stay focused and calm as I follow His direction.* No, it isn't always that easy, but when I ask Him for help and listen and wait, He answers in His own way and His own time . . . and things seem to work out.

We all need a sense of stability, and we need to recognize its source. It doesn't come from other people or from finding an escape. *It comes from an inner knowing that all is well with my soul, even when chaos surrounds me.* Impossible? No, not with a strong faith in God, and a dependence on His changeless truth.

I've noticed many issues of balance where we lean from one end to the other, like a teeter-totter, needing to find a more "equal" perspective. Determination to achieve one's own goals versus seeking God's will is one. Justice vs. compassion is another. Self-centeredness vs. concern for others. Companionship vs. solitude, courage vs. fear, humility vs. arrogance, work or play, humanity or spirituality. Working women must constantly balance financial and emotional demands (work vs. family), along with personal desires (horses, for example!). *We must seek the overall picture instead of only here and now.* We need to embrace both joy and sadness.

Miss Swift once explained that wrong posture can feel right, when it's a habit. To make changes, one must learn to "feel" the right way. I had ridden for years without lessons and it was difficult to change how my body sat and moved on a horse. With time, effort, and the help of several different instructors over the years, I tried to make changes. I'm still working on it.

We could go through all of life with bad habits that seem right, if we never learn a better way. If someone who knows better should have the opportunity, and we would listen, we could learn that many things should be changed! *Sometimes it takes a crisis or a painful event to reveal the need for change.* Our spiritual beliefs as well as our daily habits may have unrecognized error (Add to the "teeter-totter" list: An open mind vs. a steadfast belief . . . steadfast belief is good only when based on truth!).

We may believe the saying, "The Lord helps those who help themselves," because we have heard it many times . . . but it isn't biblical! Scripture teaches us to "Trust in the Lord with all your heart and lean not on your own understanding; in all your ways acknowledge Him, and He will make your paths straight." (Proverbs 3:5–6)

Sometimes I feel frustrated and overwhelmed by too many "shoulds." I can't do everything for everyone and I'm not supposed to! That's when I need to reconsider my balance. Needs vs. wants. My will or God's . . . or is it really the will of someone else? Trying to "fix" everyone's problems is at one end of the scale vs. having concern only for oneself. The shoulds find their proper place as I balance the "teeter-totter."

Some mornings, overwhelmed by conflict and pressures, I have wanted to stay in bed rather than face the day ahead. There have been other mornings when I awoke with a wonderful sense of God's Presence, ready for life's challenges! But life's challenges and difficulties don't come only when we're ready to meet them. The world's catastrophes don't happen at opportune moments. We need to work at keeping our physical and spiritual balance as we move on with life wherever it takes us. One word for that balance is a strong *faith* that can support and sustain us whatever happens. We move on more easily through life's obstacles because of that faith.

Fanny came into my life when I most needed a horse. I was feeling trapped and lonely, with a need for self-worth. During twenty years of marriage, I tried to be a submissive wife. I was active in our church. I had always wanted a horse, but there was no money or time to follow that dream. In the two years before we bought Fanny, my grandmother died, we moved away from my closest friendships, a terrific job, and a very special church. Wes didn't seem to have a problem with all these changes and he was too busy to help me deal with it.

As I helped Mark with Fanny's training and care, I ached inside to own her myself. When I did, three years later, I found myself becoming obsessed with this new interest. Fanny became a consuming challenge and a special companion . . . my escape and my solution. Riding and training Fanny, I felt like a new person . . . more alive, more confident! I enjoyed grooming her until her coat was shiny and clean. She responded to my care and attention with true devotion. I felt I was accomplishing something I wanted!

I usually fed Fanny before getting supper. I was told that horses should be fed on schedule and I wanted to get that chore done before dark so I could spend the rest of the evening inside. My husband wanted me to fix our meal first, even though he never ate on schedule. He often accused me of putting Fanny ahead of the family.

Wes also felt I spent more time with Fanny than with our sons. The boys were teenagers now and they weren't home that much. They jogged daily to stay in shape and most of their track meets were daytime events, while I was at work. Every time I wanted to enjoy a special horse activity, some family event was scheduled that same day, or Wes planned a family trip. There was always a conflict between what I wanted to do and what the family wanted to do, and the family came first, of course. I rode the competitive rides only two weekends each year. We didn't have extra money and the boys always needed things for school. I felt guilty for wanting something for myself. I didn't feel I had the right to demand things; but I was quite good at playing the role of a not-so-silent martyr.

My father-in-law strongly believed that "Christians shouldn't have horses." I definitely didn't agree with him, and we often felt the conflict of our differing opinions. I understood the basis for his belief, but God gave man dominion over the animals He created. Didn't that mean He also gave us the responsibility for their care? I realized later that this man's opposition to animals might have come from the many problems with his own animals on the farm. I doubt that he ever experienced a really good relationship with a cow or a dog or horse, as I had.

My dad expressed his own concerns. "It's not that I don't like horses; but every time you get attached to one of them, something happens." His comment helped me understand his feelings, and my later experiences proved the validity of his words.

The family conflict became strong enough that I again turned to counselors for advice. I was told to get rid of the horse and learn to be a better wife and mother. That created even more guilt, because I couldn't bring myself to give Fanny up. I felt out of place in this family of men just as I had felt while growing up when all my friends had a mother and I didn't.

Because of Fanny, I now had friends who shared my interests. It was a welcome change to be able to talk about horses. Life was interesting and fun and I felt happier and more alive than I had ever felt before. Wes had never learned how to make a woman feel good about herself. Embarrassed with expressing deep feelings, he joked about a woman's place in the home and how he wanted an obedient wife!

When I took the matter one morning to a women's Bible study group, asking for prayer to help me know what to do, one young woman looked me straight in the eye and said very thoughtfully, "I've always believed God puts these things in us for a reason." God bless that woman . . . she gave me hope! *Maybe I wasn't so terrible after all.*

I knew my priorities were out of balance, and I wanted things to be right. But if God had put this love of horses within me, then He surely had a purpose in doing so. From then on, I looked for the reason that God might have given me this love of horses. What could I possibly do with it that would glorify Him?

I sometimes think God brought Fanny for emotional therapy. At one time, I could name five major stresses in my life, which according to my doctor could cause severe health problems within a few years. He recommended I ride as much as possible. Many times, I walked away from major conflict that I could do nothing about, to go ride. Riding somehow drained away my tension and gave me new strength and hope. Fanny's eager spirit helped me find my own joy. As long as she was sound, I was happy!

Back then, I felt a strong drive to compete with Fanny to win a competitive ride. Conditioning a horse for a thirty-mile ride took extra time and attention, special feed supplements, and liniment. For each ride, there was an entry fee and the cost of gas. I entered only two or three rides a year, however, while many riders competed almost every weekend. How did they get away from their families? How could they afford that many rides? How did their families deal with a woman having a life of her own?

When conditioning a horse for distance riding, my priorities are of course quite different than when simply enjoying a weekend trail ride. Pam's standards were geared for serious competition. But when riding goals do not reach that level, where do you cut corners? How does one determine if the goal is worth the sacrifice?

Is competition and winning really that important? Perhaps it is as important as my heart believes it is at the moment, which can change as I go through life. I no longer feel the obsession to spend time and energy conditioning a horse for a stressful ride. I no longer feel a great need to prove that my horse and I can win a prize. As I get older, I find less courage to take risks. And less need to prove my worth.

Riding my horse is still an important part of my life. It still relieves tension and helps me enjoy the beauty of nature. There is something about the good response of a horse to a human, about the touching of the animal's body, about the soothing motion of riding, something about the eagerness of my horse to go with me where I want to go. I hope as civilization continues to change, that it recognizes the need for horseback riding and areas for such riding. We need safe areas with natural beauty . . . and so much of that is being lost each year!

My experiences with Fanny taught me not only about winning a competitive ride, but winning the game of life. I had been too protected as a child. I needed to learn to make my own decisions and take responsibility for my actions and personal beliefs. I also needed to learn how to love and take care of myself, not selfishly, but realistically accepting God's purpose for me. I talked to Pam a lot about my situation. She offered some wise thoughts.

"You think you're doing good just because you're staying," she said. "But what about your attitude?" She was right. I thought I was being a good Christian because I stayed in my marriage. I was feeding my self-righteous image. But I was not being a good wife in some ways, because I didn't really want to be there, the way things were.

I seriously considered divorce, and for six months I lived in my own apartment. I enjoyed the freedom and the peace of being on my own for the first time in my life! I usually hated winter's cold, but one morning I found myself joyfully cleaning the snow off my truck windshield before going to work. That day, I felt good about myself! I had hope for new opportunities and the freedom to choose alternatives.

One evening, while Christmas shopping at a local mall, I enjoyed the beauty of a light snowfall swirling lazily around the streetlights. I stood

there in the parking lot for a long time, just looking up at the light, at the large snowflakes drift-
ing around the tall light fixture's glow and sifting
down to my face, aware of the great wonder of
this quiet moment. *I was exploring the freedom
to even be able to enjoy it!*

I received letters from my sister-in-law and
phone calls from my brother-in-law, and my
mother-in-law also had a few comments, all based
on Scripture. In spite of signed divorce papers
and a paid lawyer, I agreed to attend a "marriage encounter weekend" in early December of
1978. During the weekend's closing ceremony, I
felt God asking me to forgive Wes. With God's
help, I did; and for three days, Wes and I enjoyed a closer relationship. When I told Wes I
wanted to come back and try again, his sudden
anger puzzled me . . . and the closeness I'd felt
during those three days vanished.

When I did move back, in March of 1979, I
believed it was what God wanted, even though
Wes did not seem eager to have me return. I told
myself he was still hurting because I had left and
God would help us work through this. With God's
help, I didn't fight back when Wes got angry. But
several months later, I got tired of trying to be
the sweet, obedient wife in all things. I couldn't
be totally obedient when I disagreed so strongly
with so many of his decisions!

In 1980, I decided to quit my job. My dad had been seriously injured and I wanted to spend some time with him. I also felt I could work on my marriage if I was home more and I could try freelance writing at home.

Wes was not happy with my decision to quit work. I rode Fanny more than ever that year, enjoying two competitive rides. We had a huge garden and a big house, several cows, about one hundred chickens and two horses. Our boys were busy with school and their 4-H projects. I worked in the garden and canned a few hundred quarts of vegetables. I helped take care of all the animals, but I wasn't making any money to help pay the bills!

I remember asking God if we should sell Fanny and Dude. Soon afterward, we experienced an actual tornado! After the storm passed, almost everything was damaged except the big barn, where I had put the horses just a few hours earlier. Normally, I would have left the horses outside, in the small lot beside the barn, where they could go in and out of the lean-to . . . but I had heard the storm warnings. Now the lean-to roof was gone, the fence was down, and a power line pole lay across the lot. The horses were safe inside the big barn. I found my response in Psalm 36:6–7: "O Lord, You preserve both man and beast. How priceless is your unfailing love!"

My dad died of a sudden heart attack in March of 1981. He had been my main source of encouragement, except for Pam. I spent a lot of time that summer going back and forth from our Illinois farm to Dad's place in Iowa, settling his estate. I was also enrolled in the real estate course that Wes had encouraged me to take. That was the year that Fanny and I entered three competitive trail rides, one of which was our last. I wasn't taking enough time in the saddle to get Fanny in condition. It was time to let go of my dream of winning.

Dad left me a little money, and I used it to pay a breeding fee. I had Fanny bred to an Appaloosa stallion with quality bloodlines, hoping to continue her wonderful spirit and heart in a body with better conformation and a happier temperament. I paid five hundred dollars for the stud fee, waited eleven months and almost worried myself sick waiting . . . for what turned out to be a false pregnancy! Although I tried for several years to get Fanny re-bred, she never had another foal. Mark was now in college and I kept Dude. Dude was quieter and easier to train, but I preferred to ride Fanny.

I was still searching for a reason why God had put within me this love for horses. I still didn't see it. It didn't occur to me then that He would give me this pleasure in life simply as a gift of His love. But He had already begun to teach me the priceless lessons of partnership and submission within the horse and rider experience. He was getting ready to reveal an even more priceless message about my relationship with Him.

CHAPTER 16

A Stable Idea

*I*n 1983, Wes was transferred to the St. Louis area. While he lived in an apartment, I stayed on the farm, waiting for it to sell, and spent many weekends in the St. Louis area looking for our next home. We had Fanny and Dude, and I was hoping for a small acreage similar to what we now had.

In 1984, after what turned out to be our last weekend of house hunting, I returned home to see Fanny standing by the barn, one front leg held forward at an unusual angle. While I was gone, our son had opened the barn door at feeding time and she ran in, her right front foot landing on the pole marking the doorway. I struggled with her unsoundness the seven remaining years of her life, consulting various veterinarians who could never pinpoint a fixable problem.

Wes and I had been unable to find an acreage we both liked for the price we could afford. I wanted to buy a modest home in town and board the horses at a stable. I wanted to be free to write instead of having to work full time. Before heading home that weekend, we stopped at a stable to arrange for boarding. The owner informed us that the stable was for sale, but they planned to move to a bigger barn next door. My husband and I looked at each other with the same idea. We toured the property, asked questions and discussed the possibilities as we headed home.

We talked about it all week and went back the following weekend to see the place once more with our realtor. We walked the entire nine acres with its wooded hillside and deep ravine. It was a beautiful place! We loved the woods, the creek, the big house and the barn with ten stalls and an indoor arena! I thought about nothing else for days. What would it be like to own a stable and board horses? Could I make a go of it? I had all kinds of ideas. I wanted to name it Tall Oaks, because of the trees and because my husband's grandmother, a very special woman, once had a dairy farm by that name.

I knew we couldn't afford this price range, and I was afraid this was an impossible dream. My husband kept encouraging me. "You want it, don't you?" he kept asking. "Then let's get it!" I had to admit I was excited at the opportunity. And Wes was always one to take advantage of any opportunity! He loved the challenge.

Our farm had not sold yet, but there was a family that wanted it as soon as they sold their home in town. We finally took their home in trade, to use for rental property. That meant we didn't have money for a down payment on the stable.

We tried for a second mortgage with the stable owner. After many negotiations with the bank and the owner, details started falling into place and we felt ready to go ahead. Surely, we would be able to make enough money from boarding to help cover the extra payments!

We moved to the boarding stable a month later, with the former owner leasing the facilities for a year while they built their new barn. I had big dreams! Tall Oaks was to be my next obsession!

I didn't find a trainer to live with us as I'd hoped, and I didn't have any boarders for several months after the barn was empty and ready for new business. I placed ads and received a few phone inquiries, but no boarders came. Eight months with an empty barn, and I was starting to panic! In October, I mentioned my situation to an acquaintance at a competitive ride . . . and she knew someone in my area looking for a place to board.

In November, my first boarder arrived. A family with four children had been given an older Arabian mare and they needed extra help. The eight-year-old girl had taken a year of riding lessons, but the rest of the family knew little about horses. When I learned this was a Christian family who had been praying about finding the right stable, I was even more excited! I agreed to board Syn-cere, a beautiful sixteen-year-old registered Arabian, and help the family all I could. The situation soon evolved into my giving the whole family riding lessons.

I had never given riding lessons before and I had not planned to attempt such a task. My recent participation in the Sally Swift Clinic provided her basic principles as my beginning. I read books on how to ride and teach riding. I talked to riding instructors that I knew. I developed a written lesson plan and added ideas as I went along. *And I felt that God was helping all the way*. It was an exciting time!

For several months, I worked with this family, until the father was transferred. They decided to sell Syn-cere for one thousand dollars.

Several prospective buyers came, but she did not sell during the two months they were getting ready to move. She had been a brood mare most of her life, and was still quite green when it came to riding.

I had fallen in love with this feisty mare. There was no way we could afford one thousand dollars, and I knew that all too well. Each time someone came to look at Syn-cere, I felt a twinge of envy. When they left without her, I must admit I felt relieved.

I remember the Wednesday morning call from her owners who had been awake for hours worrying about what to do. They would sell Syn-cere to me for three hundred dollars if I could tell them yes right now. They didn't want to worry any longer. *Only three hundred dollars!* Surely I could get that much somehow! *I said yes!* That very afternoon, my mother dropped in unexpectedly for a visit, saw Syn-cere running and playing in her paddock by the barn, and agreed to loan me one hundred fifty dollars. I used that as a down payment. Three years later, it was Syn-cere that won a Fifth Place ribbon in a competitive trail ride.

Soon after acquiring Syn-cere, a friend of her former owner came for riding lessons. Since there seemed to be a real market for children wanting riding lessons, I bought a pony named Gambler (the only horse I ever owned that paid for his keep)! Gambler was a POA, a small Appaloosa, nicely marked and well-mannered.

Fanny turned out to be a good lesson horse for older beginners. She was sound enough for walk and trot, and she was smooth and reliable. The exercise actually seemed good for her. I felt guilty as I watched heavy teenagers bouncing on her back and yanking on her mouth and I tried to help them improve their skills. They didn't mean to hurt her. One sensitive boy would often tell Fanny how sorry he was whenever he realized his hands had been too strong. Fanny "got even" in her own way. She often took advantage of this young man's lack of control by grabbing a bite of hay from nearby stacked bales as she came around a corner of the barn.

Fanny surprised me at times. One day a teenage girl was trying to put the bridle on Fanny, who usually took the bit very cooperatively. This particular day, Fanny playfully ducked her head just as Autumn held the bridle in place. Autumn giggled and tried again. Fanny again ducked her head just as Autumn tried to present the bit. It became a game as Fanny ducked and Autumn giggled. I don't think Fanny was that playful with anyone else at any other time. I wondered at that; did Fanny sense Autumn's need for more fun in her life?

Many years later, in a different arena, I watched Fanny giving her gentlest trot to trusting little girls whose feet couldn't reach the stirrups. Some of those girls were my nieces and some the children of a friend. Fanny had become quite a baby-sitter. But at the same time, she let other horses in the pasture know she was still the boss mare!

I gave lessons at my stable for two years, and by then my ten stall barn was full, with four horses of my own and six boarders. I owned Fanny, Dude, Syn-cere and Gambler. I spent mornings cleaning stalls and listening to radio ministers who strengthened and comforted me through the trials and struggles. Our financial situation was getting more critical all the time, but the possibilities kept me going. Looking back on those mornings in the barn, I realize now that God fed me a rich banquet from His Word through those radio pastors! And I still feel blessed for that education in spite of the problems.

One of those radio ministers, Charles Stanley, said if a woman doesn't learn to submit to her husband, she will look for a man she can submit to. I found myself doing just that. Does a woman *need* to give herself to a man? Must a man learn to take charge in a way that his wife accepts, in order to gain willing submission? Wes seemed to ask things that always made me feel, "I don't want to!" I wanted to be a submissive wife . . . I wanted a happy partnership . . . but it was more like a constant struggle!

Charles Stanley also cautioned listeners to never allow yourself to get too hungry, too angry, too lonely, or too tired. Such conditions weaken us, opening the door for temptation to overpower us. He said to continually renew your mind with Scripture and stay focused on God's power and direction. His words were wise and true. I did feel too lonely, too tired of the struggle, too hungry for someone to connect with and perhaps too angry at God for not fixing my marriage when I had prayed for it for too many years.

Three years after we bought the stable, I was beginning to feel we could make it. I designed a special ad for a program of lessons for new horse owners. A few more months, and I really thought we could catch up. Suddenly, the former owner foreclosed on the second mortgage and actually bought back the stable. We had only a few days to pack up and get out.

In the midst of the tremendous turmoil of those few days, I felt the weight of failure. I had hoped this would be a good business, but I had probably been too timid, and too easy on un-paying boarders. We had taken on more than I could handle, just as I had feared in the beginning. On the other hand, I had learned much about horses and about riding, and I had grown spiritually as well. *God mercifully removed us from the situation, giving us the opportunity to make a new start.*

I moved three horses to another stable and sold Gambler. We settled into a cheap rental home and started to catch up on bills. Once again I had to "center . . . and grow" at a point of transition. I had to sort things out, get back in touch with my Source of energy and strength, and find a new direction for my life.

Sometimes I wonder why God has given me so much of His attention. Perhaps He did so because I needed it. Perhaps He did so because I was willing to receive it. And perhaps it was merely because of His great love. As I learn to see life from a wider perspective, I find greater peace within. I can wake up thankful to be alive, and look forward to a better future in spite of present trouble.

I thought again about the issue of balance. I realized how much a family situation can be out of balance and you don't see it . . . because you're used to it. As you see how other families are, or find help from counselors, you begin to see areas of concern. One of my marriage counselors told me, "Your marriage relationship is detrimental to your family in every way . . . physically, spiritually, and socially." I didn't realize how right he was until twenty years later, when our boys were having marriage problems of their own.

Many years after leaving the stable, I rode one day with a former boarder who asked how things were going. Grinning, she said, "You were so miserable that you made everyone around you miserable!" That made me stop and think! I had shared my problems with everyone, hoping for an answer. But no one else could solve my problem for me . . . I had to find my own answer.

Only God sees ahead, and only God knows how to avert problems and unnecessary trials. Why, then, don't we follow Him and listen to His quiet voice that tries to keep us on the right path in life? *Why do we instead follow our own ideas and plans . . . when we know we cannot see the future as He can?* We often assume that things will work out the way we want, but we have no way of knowing what will happen.

Only God knows the future. And He is willing to guide us . . . if we are willing to follow. But He does not usually take the reins and direct us forcefully as we do our horses. His gentle Spirit gives direction when we seek it and are ready to listen!

Christ tells us in Matthew 6:33 to "seek first his kingdom and his righteousness, and all these things will be given to you as well." Belonging to God's Kingdom because I have accepted Jesus Christ and the teachings of His Word, my relationship with Him should be my first priority. It is His righteousness and glory, not my own, that I should seek. When I submit to that, He takes care of the rest.

CHAPTER 17

Developing a Secure Seat

An instructor once told me that the rider's first goal in any riding discipline should be to develop a secure seat.

A "good seat" isn't a simple matter of staying in the saddle with strong leg muscles. *True security is supple stability.* Assuming the horse is not opposing the rider's place upon his back, a secure seat involves good balance and the correct use of appropriate leg muscles, while maintaining correct body position with relaxed, free moving joints. The rider should cultivate a feel for timing and the ability to stay in harmony with, or "follow," the horse's movement.

Some instructors require their students to begin riding without reins. This should only be done with a trained horse under an instructor's control. As the horse moves through various gaits on a lunge line, the student develops his riding muscles and concentrates on body position and balance. The rider may be asked to ride without stirrups, or told to reach up and out with his arms or to touch parts of the horse's body. These exercises help the student realize the great freedom of motion that is possible even while staying securely in the saddle. *Such exercises also help develop the relaxed flexibility of the rider's body that is so essential to good riding.*

Learning to ride without using the reins for support, the rider cannot injure the horse's mouth or spoil the horse's training. He learns to use his hands independently from the other aids. The Spanish Riding School gave daily lunge line training for at least three years without reins! For a serious rider, the results are worth the time, but most students become discouraged and bored spending that much time on one issue.

Riding lessons are more often begun at a walk and continued on through the trot and canter as the student is able to handle each gait comfortably. The student must cope with balance and control of his own body in response to the horse's movements, learning to apply the various aids for riding, plus the control of the horse . . . all at one time. For many new riders, this is over-whelming, not to mention a bit confusing at times for the horse. Starting out on the lunge line without reins seems in comparison much easier!

Without lessons, many people grip the horse with their lower leg, especially when riding English, as though they were riding bareback, often pointing toes outward. Some riders lean forward too far, causing their feet to go back under them with toes pointing downward. In a Western saddle, they may push their feet too far forward into the stirrups, bracing their back against the cantle of the saddle, or they may turn their feet out, pushing into the stirrups for support. The correct posture, of course, is none of the above.

Not having any lessons, I had developed my own unique style, incorporating several wrong habits. It felt right to me because I was used to it. I'd been on several competitive rides, and I felt quite secure in my Western saddle, even when partially standing in the stirrups for long periods. When I started riding in an English saddle, that was a different story! Helpful instructors tried to modify my riding style with a few lessons and I discovered how difficult it is to break old habits. *In order to change, I had to learn to feel the correct way, practicing until the right way felt right and the wrong way felt wrong.* I needed the correction and encouragement of a full time riding instructor! I needed constant reminders, to keep practicing it the correct way.

Miss Swift's principles helped me the most. First, I leaned back and forth to find my point of balance, concentrating on my imaginary center of energy. Remembering to "center and grow" helped me relax and correct my balance as needed. I imagined the weight of my relaxed torso over the horse's center of gravity, which is the lowest part of his back, just behind the withers. I felt my upper body lifting within rather than stretching up with tightened muscles . . . like a tree that grows tall, lifting in my imagination, straight and soft and light. I let my legs hang down, heavy and long, with hips open and relaxed, feeling the depth of my seat and my weight on my seat bones. I tried to imagine a straight line from my ear down through my shoulder and hip to my heel.

I concentrated on staying balanced but relaxed with soft, close contact all along the upper thigh. One of my instructors insisted that knees should be tight against the saddle, but Miss Swift cautioned not to grab too tight. Since the knees are usually above the widest part of the horse's body, too much pressure could push you up out of the saddle. Knees should not be "pinched," she said. Good balance with soft contact along the upper thighs to the knees is usually sufficient. Knees should be heavy and flexible, never stiff, allowing the upper part of the lower leg to come just below the widest part of the horse's body with the same soft contact. *Since horses' bodies and human legs are not always the same size, one should understand the principle as well as the rule.*

At a sitting trot, Miss Swift prefers the knees to be free enough to slide slightly forward with each stride . . . left, right . . . with the motion of the horse. When jumping, however, it is especially important to keep the knees securely snug against the saddle and the heels down.

Although various instructors have dissimilar ideas, the differences often depend on individual experiences with different riding disciplines or different horses. Teachers usually agree that a rider must "keep those heels down!" The correct length of stirrup is essential for comfort, security, and good riding posture . . . but this can vary, for example, with jumping and racing. The ankle should be flexible and never locked or stiff, and toes should point forward, only slightly out.

Maintaining a correct riding posture means learning to move with your horse. At a walk, you can sit quite straight in the saddle, but feel a sense of moving forward. If you sit too straight and rigid or lean back, you could be caught off guard and pulled back in the saddle if your horse changes speed suddenly. At the faster gaits of trot and canter, you can lean forward just a little to stay in balance with your horse.

With a sitting trot, I learned to move my seat with the horse with a side to side swaying rhythm, rolling my seat under, forward and down . . . pushing down into the stirrups, heel down, with a flexible ankle joint. A Western riding friend said to imagine walking in the stirrups, pushing down one foot then the other in step with the horse's rhythm. This suggestion helped some. Any such movements, however, must be very subtle and natural, never overdone.

Posting the trot was easier, as I let the movement of the horse lift me up and slightly forward with every other stride, pivoting from the knees. Keeping my balance consistent was the difficult part. I had to constantly correct my posture and reach down with legs and heels. My seat is influenced by the regularity of my horse's gait. It is more difficult to maintain balance if the horse is not consistent in rhythm.

It is easier to tell someone else how to sit and balance properly than it is to overcome years of wrong habits and attitudes that influence one's own posture.

I remember teaching a teenage boy how to ride . . . emphasizing the importance of sitting quiet and straight, balancing with legs feeling long and joints relaxed and supple. "Let the horse do the work," I told him. "Learn to feel yourself moving with him. Give to the horse's motion; don't resist it by holding your body rigid. You actually have better control when you learn to move in closer harmony with your horse."

At that moment, I realized another parallel. I often struggled to do things the "right" way and perhaps my mindset was too rigid. It would be easier to let God's Holy Spirit do His work and to learn to move with Him . . . to "follow" His will and focus on His guidance instead of struggling so much on my own to figure things out.

But how could I let God totally direct my life and still work toward my own goals, I wondered? Couldn't I have any plans or goals of my own? I have a serious responsibility for my life . . . so how can I also give up control?

My own words came back to me, "You have better control when you learn to move in harmony." It became clear. I had to be sure my personal goals were lined up in harmony with His goals! It's easy to be human and self-centered and it often seems difficult to be "spiritual!" *The key is to simply listen and yield to His Spirit.* Whenever I tense up, hesitate, resist, try to force my own way, hold back, or rush ahead, I am not in harmony. I may also be hindering God's efforts. Just as stiffness in the rider's body creates resistance to the horse's movement and reduces harmony between horse and rider, my reluctance to "go with God" also creates resistance and reduces harmony.

I remembered Miss Swift's words during a clinic: "The more you relax and feel your horse's movement, the better you can ride. You have to quiet yourself and your hands and work from your center. You have to keep breathing and keep receiving the horse's movement. You must relax and move with your horse. If you become too interested in other things and you forget to receive, your body stiffens and the brilliance of the movement is lost."

I saw in her words a parallel between receiving the horse's movement . . . and receiving spiritual guidance. I knew all too well how my Christian life lost effectiveness when I became distracted by selfish pursuits and lost focus on God's direction. Just as it takes an effort of my will to sit a horse with a balanced, quiet seat and allow the horse's motion to move my body without resistance . . . it takes a decision of my will to trust God. And to keep on trusting, day after day after day.

It's my *attitude* that God is working on here, not horsemanship! Seeing the parallel, however, between the principles of Christian living and the principles of riding somehow helps me understand both more clearly. Did God plan this analogy? Or does everything seem related simply because of a mutual Creator?

My security when riding a horse depends primarily on my *position* in the saddle. To summarize, that *position* is influenced by balance, flexibility of body and joints, development of riding muscles, sensitivity to the horse's movement and reactions, awareness of possible situations and knowledge of ways to avoid problems, my concentration, or focus, on my horse and my riding, and even my attitude toward my horse. Not to mention the horse's possible whim to unseat me!

Feelings of security may not be dependable. I may feel secure just before my horse spooks at a newspaper blowing in the wind and dumps me! A rider needs to develop an awareness of possibilities and be ready to prevent problems . . . or perhaps choose to not ride on windy days!

I may feel I'm okay spiritually, but can I be sure? Scripture teaches that we can know we have spiritual security. *God's Word says my spiritual security depends on my position "in Christ," not on my feelings.* The actual security of my eternal future depends on my "positional" relationship with Jesus Christ, the Son of God, based on my acceptance of His Sovereign authority, by a decision or a commitment.

My *feelings* of security may be influenced by how well I balance my prayer life with Bible study and fellowship with other Christians, on my flexibility to changes that God allows in my life, and my sensitivity and obedience to the leading of the Holy Spirit. My feelings also depend on the depth of my relationship with God, my faith in His power and love, and the attitude of my heart toward Him. *But my actual eternal security depends totally on what Jesus has already done and nothing more (His crucifixion was the ultimate sacrifice for all sin . . . past, present and future).*

Spiritual security is just as fundamental as a secure riding seat. I had always believed in God, but I was raised in a church that didn't help me feel secure. Visiting a different church with a different message, I finally discovered the security I had longed for. *The experience of my decision to accept Jesus as my Savior gave me assurance of a new life "in Christ."* Life itself has no guarantees, no absolute security. But God's Word tells how to find a secure position based on trust in His absolute love.

Old habits are difficult to overcome. My old nature provided no inner security in times of crisis, and I had to learn to go beyond the past, beyond feelings. I was too dependent on others for support, for advice, for encouragement. *I had to learn to trust God's Word as the basis for my security and Christ's death on the cross as the reason for that security.* I had to trust those facts more than feelings and learn to rely on Christ more than my own understanding.

With Christ as my true security, it doesn't matter what else changes. I'm still learning that all of my struggles and fears, my disappointments and failures, cannot hurt my position in Christ. *That position is secure because He is faithful.* I am His and He has promised to provide my needs and be with me always.

I remember a moment of crisis, when I asked, "Where do I go from here?" In answer, I seemed to hear Miss Swift's reminder to "center and grow!" And I tried to center again upon Jesus Christ and His Word and to grow from my experience. That reminder has given me hope and direction at many turning points in my life.

Centering on Christ brings peace. I meditate on who He is and what He can do. I remember His faithfulness, even when I've strayed. *I remind myself that God's grace does not depend on my feelings or my performance, but on Christ's death on the cross.* I remember how I worked to change Fanny's focus from self-direction to listen to my leadership. Was God doing the same with me?

I wanted to be a good rider who never came out of the saddle. Instead, I learned to climb back up after a fall and try again. Wanting to be perfect, I tried to base my security on my performance. But Scripture says that all have sinned, and I am included.

Sin has consequences even when forgiven. Sin has sometimes affected my fellowship with God, but it hasn't ended the relationship. Instead, God showed me His tremendous love and mercy. I learned the true security of my position in Christ was based on His righteousness, not mine. Here Fanny was another model for me: Though she was far from perfect, I loved her anyway!

With my security in Christ, I can reach out for life's opportunities with greater courage. I can take risks and trust His love and provision. Where He leads, He will provide a way. I don't need to depend on this world's wealth or cling to man's traditions. I can rely on God's strength and wisdom, not just my own. I am finding the freedom to make mistakes as I search for answers and I can meet life's failures with less despair. When I fall, I can take His hand and He helps me up so I can go on. His acceptance gives me freedom to be myself, and be honest about my fears, feelings, and needs. I am God's child, not because I deserve it or because I have earned it, but because He is a loving Father who has loved, accepted, and adopted me.

I once believed my goal in life was to get to Heaven, and I lived in fear of missing it. God assured me one morning that His Son had met that goal for me. *My acceptance of Christ's atonement gave me a secure seat in God's Kingdom with a new purpose.* I could stop struggling to be good enough to go to Heaven and learn to live to glorify Him. Even as an imperfect human being, I can glorify God with a thankful spirit of worship, content with what He has given me.

I am encouraged by the words that Jesus spoke in John 10: 27–29: "My sheep listen to my voice; I know them, and they follow me. I give them eternal life, and they shall never perish; no one can snatch them out of my hand. My Father, who has given them to me, is greater than all; no one can snatch them out of my Father's hand."

According to Paul in Ephesians, we are seated with Christ, in Heaven, if we belong to Him. "But because of his great love for us, God, who is rich in mercy, made us alive with Christ even when we were dead in transgressions—it is by grace you have been saved. And God raised us up with Christ and seated us with him in the heavenly realms in Christ Jesus." (Ephesians 2:4–6)

No seat is more secure than that!

CHAPTER 18

Working on the Bit

The memory of one splendid moment lingers in vivid detail inside my mind. I am riding Fanny in the outdoor arena and she briefly consents to tuck her head obediently, arching her cresty neck and showing off her most springy slow collected trot. With only a gentle contact with the bit, I can feel her energy and strength in my hands. *It is an incredible delight to experience her power under my control, even for a few minutes! It is a moment of jubilant triumph and a humbling gift!*

Though she was not totally sound those last few years, she was still full of that "wonderful go-juice" as Pam once described it. She had achieved a wonderful collected canter previously, but if I asked for her right lead now, she would soon be quite lame. Her collected trot still had amazing lightness and power. Maintaining her collection was, however, like resisting an accommodating giant with a single finger. Fanny allowed such restraint only so long; then she'd throw her head up and stretch out her nose, pulling the reins through my hands. In that moment of freedom, she would burst forth with exuberant speed until I could regain control. Years of 4-H speed events and competitive riding had reinforced her natural tendency . . . she loved to run!

Fanny never did learn to work on the bit consistently, like the Arab I watched in the Coliseum. She was so eager and headstrong, so full of energy most of the time that my efforts to slow her down often resulted in an excited rebellion!

In my desire to avoid this rebellion, I searched for a greater understanding of this principle of "working on the bit." Culminating my research into one sentence, I would describe it basically as a willing, submissive attitude in the horse, revealed in a collected body frame, ready to move in any direction the rider asks. This is not a picture of a "deadhead," mind you! This is an animal with power and energy and ability!

Using equal light pressure on both reins, the rider strives to maintain a gentle contact with the horse's mouth through the bit. A horse should flex at the poll, the head positioned with a vertical line from the eyes to the nose. Holding the bit in his mouth, the horse should feel the slightest pressure from the rider's hands and respond willingly and quickly. *More than form and control, working on the bit is a matter of mutual respect and cooperation . . . an embodiment of intimate partnership between horse and rider.* It is the "ideal" more than common reality, except for higher levels of dressage, perhaps, and it usually results only from years of horse and rider working together through various levels of communication, trust, and ability.

Fanny typically held her nose out in front, which is called being "ahead of the bit." If she had brought it in tight to her chest, she would have been "behind the bit." Both are ways a horse avoids the rider's use of the bit as communication and control.

I must admit I had a fetish about wanting Fanny to tuck her head for me. I loved the look of it, but that gracefully tucked head and curved neck was an indicator to me of her willing compliance in our partnership. And once I actually knew the feeling of her body under me poised in balanced collection, it became a fascinating goal!

I have watched trainers put a horse "on the bit" in one easy lesson, it seemed! But to me, it is a more progressive communication, refined throughout a horse's training. A younger horse is able to give to the bit a little at a time, when asked to turn, stop, back up, and go forward. After the horse learns to respond to gentle pressure, the trainer can gradually ask for greater submission as the horse is ready to give it.

Just like a child, a horse needs encouragement and praise for every try. He must learn what the rider wants, and he must be willing to cooperate and focus on the job. A horse will not feel submissive every day, just as people have days when we don't feel like doing what we should! That doesn't mean we don't ask for more . . . but we are persistent with understanding. We patiently work to keep the horse's attention and cooperation.

The rider's greatest challenge may be to obtain *consistent* willingness! The rider must not overwork his horse too often or make demands that the horse is unable to meet. The horse should respect and trust his rider and not be afraid of being hurt by what he is asked to do. A trainer needs to consider a horse's physical limitations as well as his mental abilities. His neck muscles, for instance, cannot hold a new position for long periods of time without strain. Collection itself is a strain on many parts of the body. After a collected canter, it's kind to let him walk with the reins loose for a few minutes.

Wherever a horse's conformation is less than perfect, that area may show greater weakness under hard use. If a horse has had an injury, or his muscles are tired or sore from stress, it is possible that collection and turning can cause further injury if the horse is ridden improperly.

A rider who asks too much of her horse may later have to deal with a reluctant or sour attitude. A horse can't tell us his problems, so it's up to us to "listen" to his horsey ways of moving and resisting. The horse's attitude of eager submission is a fragile entity the trainer should protect and nurture as a precious reward for his time and patience. In the book *My Horses, My Teachers* by Alois Podhajsky, the author observes, "Thus I realised the meaning of collection, which might be compared to the mental concentration of a human being."[1] He learned from his horses, just as they learned from him. He had great respect for these magnificent creatures and was willing to "listen" to their needs and abilities as he trained.

---

[1] Podhajsky, Alois. *My Horses, My Teachers*. (Trafalgar Square Publishing, North Pomfret, Vermont 05053, 1997) page 60.

Pam had that kind of sensitivity, to feel what a horse needed and what he could do. For three months, she learned from Colonel Podhajsky himself. Pam often cautioned me to ride with gentle hands. Constant pulling and hard pressure dulls the sensitivity of the horse's mouth, she said. My problems with Fanny had proved that!

The successful partnership of horse and rider is a relationship of mutual submission based on countless interrelated factors. The rider should be as skilled as possible to bring out the best from a horse. The concept of working on the bit involves constant connection with the rider. Maintaining gentle contact with the horse's mouth through the bit involves several aspects of body control . . . including a secure, balanced seat for a foundation that does not hinder the use of the hands, a supple body with relaxed joint movement, and gentle hands that can follow the movement of the horse's head without inflicting discomfort.

When I have gentle control through close contact, I feel more connected to my horse. A tight rein causes resistance and a loose rein has little control, but gentle contact is positive communication. Instead of "control," imagine a hug. A hug that is too tight makes you want to get loose. A hug that's too loose has little meaning. An effective hug is loving, secure, and encouraging all at once . . . similar to gentle, close contact with the bit. It can communicate a sense of connection, a need to be ready for action, or a message to slow down or turn. It can say, "I am here and I am in control. Don't be afraid. I'll direct you." First, however, the rider must learn to give direction effectively.

The experience of harmony in movement with a horse, of really moving together as one, is almost beyond words of description! It is the joyful partnership of two beings, a connection both spiritual and physical, and perhaps a gift from the Creator of all life.

If I compare the principle of "working on the bit," with a relationship between God and man called "walking in the Spirit," I see an amazing parallel. "Walking in the Spirit" is a moment-by-moment surrender to God's leadership, an advanced spiritual discipline just as working on the bit is an advanced discipline in horsemanship.

When a person acknowledges God's Sovereignty and enters into a personal relationship with Jesus Christ, the Scriptures teach that the Holy Spirit comes to live within that person. The Spirit is a helper, a private tutor who works to maintain close fellowship. Just as a rider uses the aids of hands, bit, body, and leg . . . the Spirit works through the aids of God's Word, daily quiet time and prayer, and sometimes people or circumstances. God has many ways of reaching out to man in His guidance.

As a new Christian, I didn't understand "walking in the Spirit." I had a strong human tendency to struggle in my own effort. I was reminded one day how becoming a Christian involves a willful act of surrender when one chooses to let God take charge. Living the Christian life, I was told, is a commitment to continue that same faith and surrender, day after day, moment by moment. I must be willing to let God direct my life, keeping an attitude of prayerful submission. As I learn to be aware of His Presence more consistently, I should be obediently sensitive to His guidance.

Here is a fascinating parallel! A Christian bows his head in prayer in reverent submission to God. The horse tucks his head and flexes at the poll in submission to his rider. A Christian is taught to accept God's Word and to hold it in his heart, to enable the Holy Spirit to use that Word to guide his life. The horse is taught to accept the bit, holding it so as to feel the pressure of guidance from the rider's hands. The horse learns to seek contact, or connection, with the rider through the bit. Man seeks connection with God through Scripture and prayer. *With horse or mankind, the guidance system's effectiveness depends on the willingness and commitment of the one accepting the other's guidance!* A horse must learn to understand the meaning of the rider's cues. A Christian must learn to understand the significance of God's Word for directing his life.

As I realized the intimate connection possible in a partnership of horse and rider, I felt God showing me a similar communion between God and man. Fanny was no longer the object of concern. *Now the pressure was on me . . . to accept God's control and learn to apply and obey what He was teaching me!*

Being somewhat headstrong like Fanny, I resisted. Fearful of what God would ask, I hesitated. But I would never know what God could do in my life . . . I would never know what my life could be . . . unless I took that step of complete submission.

I had struggled to be a better Christian, and I was frustrated by failures. I tried too hard, friends told me. But I was trying to do it *on my own*. I didn't yet understand how it worked! I still remember the morning I refused to get out of bed to go to church, too full of despair to keep on trying.

"I can't do it, God," I told Him. "I can't be the Christian everyone expects me to be! I can't be perfect and I can't change how I feel!"

And somewhere inside my head, a silent voice whispered back, *"That's what I've been waiting for! Now . . . let Me do it, through you!"*

I got up that morning with a yielded spirit and new hope. I stopped struggling to be the perfect Christian, and I let God take over a deeper level of my being. It made an unbelievably peaceful difference for several months . . . until I encountered a situation that challenged my obedience again. And I struggled once more to do things my own way.

I wanted to take responsibility for my life as a mature adult, but I wanted God to be in control. I simply couldn't comprehend how to do both at the same time. One day, as I watched a jumping clinic, I realized my answer. The horse jumps an obstacle at his rider's request, depending on his rider for direction in maneuvering the course. The horse may refuse to jump or knock down a pole. With encouragement, the horse learns to lift a little higher.

The rider has a great influence on the horse's action, but the horse is the one that clears the jump or hits a pole. *The rider works to develop the horse's skill; but in the end, the brilliance and clarity of the jump depends upon the horse.*

Several years ago, people quoted a popular phrase, "Let go and let God!" Let go of what? Not responsibility! I never accomplished anything by not trying. But when I let go of my struggle to do things my own way and let God help me do it His way, I often sensed His control as He worked things out.

We are commanded to walk in the spirit in Galatians 5:16. "So I say, live by the Spirit, and you will not gratify the desires of the sinful nature. For the sinful nature desires what is contrary to the Spirit, and the Spirit what is contrary to the sinful nature. They are in conflict with each other, so that you do not do what you want." If we follow the spirit's leading, we are in union with God's will. If we walk in the flesh, listening only to self, we tend to get off the path God has planned for us. Some say that life is a struggle of physical against spiritual. It is a continual series of choices . . . giving in to what I want . . . or giving in to what God wants.

When I accept Christ and His Holy Spirit comes to live within me, I have a "new" nature . . . the influence of the Holy Spirit. Conflict now arises . . . between old habits and the gentle pull of the new spiritual nature of God as

He works to remold my life from within. It is my dependence on the Holy Spirit that helps me live a holy life. I could never do it on my own. *I cannot be a genuine Christian without Christ living in me through the power of His Holy Spirit.*

Just as a dressage rider constantly directs and corrects the horse through leg, rein, body, and voice, God is constantly directing and correcting my life as I study His Word and pray for His guidance. I must guard the communication of that guidance, for it can easily be ignored, doubted, drowned out by worldly interests, quenched by a hardened heart or specific sin, or a stubborn will. *The communion of God's Spirit with man is a gentle touch of love, a tender guidance, and a subtle cue.* Although He has sometimes controlled circumstances of my life in ways I did not like, the quiet whisper of His Spirit has never been forceful upon my life. He has given me the choice to follow Him or to follow my own stubborn will. True wisdom lies in following Him.

In dressage, the horse is carefully trained to follow individual cues for each movement. The rider can then put those movements together into a pattern as desired. When I see a high-level dressage horse responding immediately to each subtle cue of his rider, I marvel at the beauty of this "glorious submission!" I wish others could look at my life and see the same kind of surrender in my partnership with God!

Seeing the parallel relationship of horse and rider, I can better understand God's perspective as He works in my life. A constant awareness of His Presence and His direction makes the difference between an average Christian and a victorious Spirit-filled Christian! The victorious Christian has learned to respond quickly to the subtle promptings of God's Spirit and respond with eager obedience. *His victory in living a Holy life is in his dependence on God and his joyful involvement in the partnership!*

I want to be a victorious Christian . . . not by working toward perfection and trying to live by the rules as I have in the past, but by letting God direct my life in the power of His Holy Spirit. I may never be perfect, but I can point to the One who is! I want to experience His control, to know His will for my life. I want Him to use my life to reach out to others. I want to be obedient . . . but my desire is not consistent.

My experiences with Fanny were a special gift from God, but they did not make me a perfect rider, a perfect trainer, or a perfect Christian. I will never be all that I could have been, or all that I would like to be. I will never be perfect and holy on this Earth. *But if I stop trying . . . if I stop receiving His guidance that points me in the right direction, I am no longer following His goal for my life.*

I can't change the past, but I can be open toward the future. Paul's words in Philippians 3:13b–14 are a positive reminder: ". . . Forgetting what is behind and straining toward what is ahead, I press on toward the goal . . ."

God has shown me that He is the goal. "For it is God who works in you to will and to act according to his good purpose." (Philippians 2:13) The Grand Prix level dressage horse did not train himself. He allowed his master to do it.

> *Dear Lord, help me to eagerly allow Your guidance! Help me overcome my reluctance, my resistance, my doubts and fears . . . anything that hinders my total commitment to follow You! I cannot do it by myself . . . I need Your help. I want to work with You in partnership to accomplish Your will in my life!*

CHAPTER 19

Connection, Submission, and Partnership

A woman needs a horse . . . because husbands are imperfect! Most men don't know what a woman feels or needs . . . and even when she tries to tell him, he is either too busy to listen or he doesn't take her seriously.

Horses aren't perfect, either . . . but when you have a close relationship with a horse, that horse knows how you feel. A horse knows when you are ready to take the high jump, and he will give it all that he has (but he will hesitate if you are afraid . . . because he will sense that fear even when you try to hide it!). He wades into deep waters when you ask him to go there. He stands still when you mount him, if you've told him that's what you want. Or he moves off quickly because he knows the race is important. *That's connection . . . and it's the horse's submissive nature (unlike a man's).*

Some horses take advantage, just like husbands. Others give constant loyalty, and that's the kind to have. You need a mutual trust, because trust is the basic foundation for any relationship. It is trust that prompts a horse to allow his owner to do what needs to be done, whether picking up a hoof, giving a shot or putting on a bridle. It takes more than simple trust, however, for a working relationship to develop into a special intimacy of thought, movement, and purpose. It takes time together, a special connection, agreement in purpose, mutual submission, and patience . . . a combination that can produce a magical partnership . . . in any relationship whether horse and rider or husband and wife!

The development of the cooperative partnership with a special horse is a precious experience in itself . . . similar to the blossoming of true love between two humans. *In the effort to find successful partnership, someone has to take charge and someone has to give in . . . but the outcome should be a mutual responsibility and mutual submission.* Learning each other's ways, learning to work together happily . . . isn't it the same with marriage?

Relationships aren't perfect, of course, because no being is perfect, whether horse or human! I can understand why some people prefer to be alone. Within any relationship, it is a struggle to find mutual submission . . . to give up some of one's own desires and learn to cooperate with the desires of another . . . to exercise patience, understanding, and forgiveness. I always felt a tremendous need for someone . . . for security, approval and affirmation, love, and comfort . . . someone to help take charge. I was more willing to give in than most women, but I didn't want to. My marriage did not provide the special connection I longed for. There always seemed to be a wall between us. I wanted a companion . . . someone with whom I could enjoy life. Wes was a serious work-a-holic who rarely took time for "us" to enjoy each other. He wanted a secretary . . . an obedient working partner. I wanted to feel loved and "connected."

I felt a connection with Fanny . . . a very real form of love. My adventures with Fanny gave me a sense of self worth . . . and the freedom to live a more independent, more confident life. For sixteen years, Fanny took me into a different world and helped me reach out beyond where I had been. *She gave me the sense of partnership I needed to fill my lonely place.* A woman sometimes needs a horse, just to survive in her other worlds.

As Pam and I enjoyed long, precious talks about horses and life, our friendship grew. Though Pam was younger than I was, she had taken charge of Fanny's training . . . and me as well. I envied her knowledge about horses and her confident ability with Fanny. Pam was almost always there when I needed her and she usually had an answer. I felt such a strong need for companionship that I greatly treasured these connections. Had I become more dependent upon Pam . . . than upon God?

I had other women friends before Pam and I had often called one when I needed to talk. They didn't always know how to help me, and they had their own problems. I often felt guilty for needing so much. Sometimes I felt worse after talking . . . even more unworthy and unlovable. But it was my own attitude toward myself beneath it all.

Everyone needs a relationship held firm with love. God plans for family love to secure the growth of a child, but families aren't perfect either. Sometimes we grow up with unexplained deep cravings. Proverbs 19:22 says that we desire unfailing love. Not finding it with parents, spouse, or friends, some people work to gain

money and recognition. Some people seem un-
aware of a need for others. And all the while,
God wants us to realize and enjoy His own unfailing love for each one of us.

How we interpret our needs and what we do
to meet those needs shapes our entire future. If
we could honestly express feelings and needs
without embarrassment or fear, and without
playing games, perhaps our communication
would lead to solutions. When I say, "I love you,"
I want my husband to say, "I love you" back.
Wes couldn't. Some people have been injured
emotionally and are unable to be that open to a
relationship with another person. They may feel
love without being able to express it. Relationships with parents may have lacked an example.
Specific experiences may have caused the need
to build a wall. Others are overly protective,
afraid of losing what they have.

Involvement with a horse can be a signifi-
cant beginning for someone who has retreated
into a private, protective world. Children with
various types of problems often benefit from
associations with horses. Therapeutic horsemanship programs can help participants to make
progress physically, plus enhancing a person's
ability to interact with another being. I'm sure
it's the building of connection that helps the

most. *We all need to feel we are not alone.* A special bond with a horse can open the door to better personal understanding and greater self-esteem and to healthier relationships with others. *I believe it can also point to the ultimate relationship with God Himself.*

What we all really need is the unfailing love that only God can give. Only God fully understands us, knows our past, present, and future and loves us anyway and never gives up on us. When we discover this truth, we have found the ultimate connection . . . the source of true fulfillment of all our needs. *And when we allow Him to flow His unfailing love into us and through us to others, it is a healing power for all.*

I believe that all relationships are built on similar principles. Making decisions together, one must take charge and one must give in. Lasting harmony calls for mutual responsibility and submission, however, so both parties have needs met. My husband didn't want to hear my problems . . . he was busy with his own. I felt lonely, depressed, and trapped. There were times that I desperately wanted a different life, but I never had the courage or self-worth to insist. More dependent on people (than God), I was often afraid to be on my own. Inside, I just wanted to touch someone, to have a hug.

I always believed that God brought Fanny to me for a purpose. I learned much from my experiences with her . . . techniques of working with horses, lessons for personal growth and spiritual understanding, and principles that apply to different relationships. Plus the special joy of the horse and rider connection. From the time that Fanny first came into my life, I felt God was somehow arranging the circumstances . . . and I felt that same conviction again and again, even when Fanny was taken from me. God was visibly in charge all the way . . . and I knew there had to be a purpose.

God's purpose did not culminate in training a horse or providing a friend, certainly, but in revealing my need for a more intimate relationship with my own gentle Master. *As much as I needed a husband, friends, or a horse . . . I needed His guidance and influence, His love and comfort all the more!*

Fanny was only a horse. And whatever she gave me, it ultimately came from a loving, caring Father. I haven't always felt His Presence or found immediate answers to my prayers. But in His own time and way, He has given me greater insight to grow emotionally and spiritually. I have learned that He loves me all the time, even in spite of my unfaithfulness to Him. I have learned that He can and should always be trusted completely. God is never too busy. Developing a partnership with our loving and Sovereign God is the most precious and unique experience ever!

God gives and is . . . unfailing love. He provided a covering for man's first sin. He provided a sacrifice for all of mankind, so that anyone can enter into His Presence, forgiven and justified, no matter how terrible the past. In the midst of man's sin and shame, He reaches out with compassionate love. He sees our need as well as our rebellion. He offers a new beginning . . . if only we are willing to go to Him. He offers eternal life. He offers joy and peace in place of guilt and sorrow. He even offers to help us overcome our own reluctance and lack of courage and commitment. If we ask Him.

God wants us to enter into a sincere, meaningful relationship with Him and accept Him as the Master of our partnership. He asks for our trust and our obedience. *This is perhaps the only way He can help us get from where we humanly are in life to where He knows we can and should be spiritually!*

Without this connection with God, we are on our own. Why do we seek our own will when His is so much better? Why do we turn away from the very life giving force we need? Isaiah 54:10

says 'Though the mountains be shaken and the hills be removed, yet my unfailing love for you will not be shaken nor my covenant of peace be removed,' says the Lord." According to one Bible scholar, the phrase, "unfailing love," appears in Scripture thirty-two times, always attributed to God, never a man. Romans 8:38–39 says, "For I am convinced that neither death nor life, neither angels nor demons, neither the present nor the future, nor any powers, neither height nor depth, nor anything else in all creation, will be able to separate us from the love of God that is in Christ Jesus our Lord." The only wall between God and us is the one we ourselves put there!

I believe with all my heart that God led me to Fanny, brought Pam to help with her training, and used it all to enrich my life and help me understand His Sovereign loving nature. He works in any life that will allow Him, to establish that wonderful, intimate connection that we all need. He offers unconditional love. But as He says, "I love you," He wants a personal response . . . a commitment just like in a marriage. The resulting relationship with an all-knowing, loving God is beyond our understanding at first, but the process of building such a relationship is an exciting, beautiful journey! He desires us to depend on Him more than anyone or anything else. He wants to be our God . . . our only God! He wants to hear, "I love you" back.

Depending on God leads to submission. Through all my experiences with Fanny, I learned that submission is a necessary component of an effective partnership. To some, the word submission has a bad connotation. Women bristle at the thought of submission, perhaps because we feel it is often pushed upon us a bit too strongly. A man may feel his strength and position of authority is threatened by being submissive to a woman. *Yet, we all want to be loved, and submission is a natural outcome of love.* There is a desire to give of oneself to another, and it can be glorious and uplifting. The beauty of love is in the giving to the other . . . a mutual, willing submission. If submission is demanded, it is not a giving . . . it is a taking, and the essence of love is missing. God Himself was the example of perfect love when He offered His own Son as a sacrifice on the cross for the sin of all mankind. He gave His best offering that we might enjoy His fellowship in Heaven forever.

Partnership between horse and rider grows as a decision is made by one and accepted by the other. Step by step it is built . . . a touch, a response . . . a squeeze of the rein, a giving of the jaw and neck . . . gentle leg pressure, a bend-ing of the ribcage . . . subtle cues, willing obedience . . . a rider positioning his own body correctly, learning to position the horse's body. *Each step may be small, but each step has a purpose, meaning, and place in the final outcome.*

Even so, with a man and a woman, there is a questioning look, an answering smile . . . a touch, a warm response . . . a beginning and continuing. And later, there are tough decisions and hard times . . . and there is mutual submission to each others needs and there is a strengthening of the bond . . . an increase of understanding and depth of commitment and an ever-increasing love and closeness. Or sometimes not.

A man must learn to take charge in a way his woman accepts. Otherwise, she will try to take charge herself, just as a horse will when it does not accept the rider's authority. True partnership can not exist in the midst of a struggle of wills. It is a product of connection and mutual submission . . . of coming to an agreement. It is also a product of involvement beyond physical needs, reaching into the emotional needs for security and belonging. A woman (or horse) must feel safe in submitting. As Charles Stanley warned, if a woman cannot learn to submit to her husband, she may look for a man to whom she can submit!

As imperfect human beings, we need something beyond ourselves to make us better, even though we sometimes feel a bit too sure of ourselves. And though God our Creator is a supernatural, spiritual, unseen eternal Being, holy and perfect and beyond our highest understanding, He wants an intimate relationship with each of us. *He wants us to depend on Him so He can make us better.*

Such a relationship begins and grows as God reaches out to us in love and we respond. A prayer is answered . . . a need is supplied . . . a sorrow is comforted . . . a weakness is strengthened . . . an awareness of sin leads to forgiveness and peace. *He does not ask for our perfection . . . He asks for our trust and obedience as He guides us toward it.*

God deserves our total commitment . . . our total submission . . . even though we often choose to serve ourselves instead of His high purpose. His grace and mercy responds to those who call on His name, and His wisdom and authority empowers those who humble themselves and seek His help. He is able to sustain a close connection with anyone who desires it. Some people say they don't need God. It's not a matter of being so stupid or weak that we can't make our own decisions (though we all may feel that way at times!); but just as a human has more intelligence than a horse, God has immeasurably more knowledge and wisdom than the wisest man. If you believe in the creation, that God has made this world and all that is within it . . . the majestic mountains, the glorious sunsets, the sweet song of a bird and the delicate fragrance of a rose . . . you must recognize His vast superiority and creative power!

Recognizing our human imperfection, we do want to be better, stronger, and wiser, and we strive for recognition and achievement. But God's Spirit works to convict us of our true need and draw us to the Father to experience His mercy and grace. To those who accept His Sovereign will, He sends His Holy Spirit to somehow live within us to be our connection to Himself, to be our personal guide, to strengthen and comfort us, help us through our worldly trials, and build an intimate partnership with our Creator for eternity. Just as a horse learns to accept the rider's leadership and submit to a higher will than his own, we also can learn to follow God's leadership, through His Spirit, and to live obediently to His guidance. Think seriously of the glorious results!

God is able, in spite of our human ignorance, mortal weakness and selfish desires, to work things out in the end to follow His superior plan. Scripture tells us, in Romans 8:28, "And we know that in all things God works for the good of those who love Him, who have been called according to his purpose." We are all "called" to enjoy an intimate connection with God, to work with Him toward eternal goals and values . . . to partnership with Him for everlasting time and purpose. God gives us a free will to choose to respond to His calling or ignore and refuse it. *Our choice, however, has an everlasting consequence.* If we choose not to allow His Sovereign guidance, we are on our own in a desperately wicked world. Or we struggle with it all until His persistent loving calls finally touch a receptive ear.

Don't we sometimes struggle with a certain horse until one day, hopefully, he begins to understand and give in? Then we feel that special connection and we are finally able to get somewhere and work with him in a growing partnership. It is a moment of rejoicing! When the same thing happens between God and man, the angels and all of Heaven rejoice!

During a show, we may see a splendid performance of horse and rider. Finally, all the work pays off and victory is won! But a horse must be "fit" to do the work. And a Christian must also be "fit." Sin and weakness hinders our life and its example, just as a horse's weakness, lack of training, or stamina hinders a performance in the arena.

Hebrews 3:12 warns us, "See to it, brothers, that none of you has a sinful, unbelieving heart that turns away from the living God." Later verses explain that Jesus Christ, the Son of God, is our saving high priest. Verse 16 of chapter 4 urges us, "Let us then approach the throne of grace with confidence, so that we may receive mercy and find grace to help us in our time of need."

There were many times I turned to Pam or other friends, a husband, or Fanny for companionship . . . when I should have turned first to God. Afraid to be on my own, I leaned on others . . . it was easier . . . and I was limited by their limitations and directed by their purposes. If I can't find my own inner strength, I am at the mercy of someone else's weakness! We all seek companionship to feel we are not alone. God created a woman so man would not be alone. But even when we have good relationships with husband, friends and family, and a horse . . . we still need God.

We need His peace in the midst of a world of turmoil and fearful evil. We need His comfort in times of tragedy. We need the strength that only He can give. We need His restoration . . . for only God, through Christ His Son, has provided for our eternal life in Heaven. We need to be in partnership with His Spirit, to be able to realize our true purpose and worth.

Job was a righteous man that lost everything. He told his companions, "The Lord gave and the Lord has taken away; may the name of the Lord be praised." (Job 1:21) Even when God took Fanny away from me, He compassionately worked out the details in a way that revealed His loving hand in it all. And before He took her, He provided another connection in my life.

It was at the stable where Fanny was boarded her last few years, that I met a man who became a special friend. He had purchased his first horse and I was hired to help care for that horse until he retired. I tried to teach him what I had learned about working with horses, and we rode together. Our friendship grew . . . and I found the connection I'd always wanted. At first, we joked about being soul mates. Many years later, we were married. In spite of my strong belief against divorce, I finally chose to seek happiness instead of living in misery. I chose to enjoy the mutual involvement I'd always wanted in a marriage. Instead of trying to please everyone else, I had to be true to myself. Leaving a long term relationship was extremely difficult, but my need for the connection was greater. I had to give up my image of being the "good wife" who stayed no matter what. I had to admit my own failure . . . my inability to fix everything . . . and I had to deal with a fear of losing God's favor.

I am certain now that within my personal and intimate relationship with a loving Father, knowing and trusting in that absolute love, I am finally free to be my true self no matter what that is. God loves me too much to give up on me.

The goal of training is to teach a horse to depend upon its rider. Each horse has different fears and problems from past experiences and the horse trainer works to conquer each hindrance to the "perfect" connection . . . to control and develop the horse's ability. God also works with mankind toward that same goal . . . to eliminate hindrances to a more perfect partnership. Without our dependence upon God, He cannot develop all the potential He has placed within each one of us. But . . . as we submit to His guidance and wisdom, God the Sovereign Creator has the power to give new life, hope, and glory through the indwelling of His Holy

Spirit. Through the ultimate gift of partnership with our Creator, we learn the mysteries of eternity. The learning never ends, you know.

Dear Lord, I pray that each reader will think about this idea of partnership with You and will seek to know its truth. Help us to learn to wait patiently for Your guidance and to be willing and obedient. May we learn from our horses the lessons You have placed within them for us to accept. Help us learn to focus on Your purpose above our own. Help us find the partnership with You that lifts us above human ways toward eternal glory. And may each one of us find our own vision of the message You have revealed.

CHAPTER 20

For the Love of Fanny

On my dresser is a handmade wooden horse, with three horseshoes at its base. The fourth is nailed to a fencepost at the edge of a distant field, marking the grave of a very special Appaloosa mare named Fanny.

$\mathcal{I}$t was Monday afternoon, January 28, 1991, when I received the call from the owner of the stable where Fanny was boarded.

"Betsy, you've got to come right away." I knew immediately that something had happened to

Fanny, even though I was also boarding Dude at the same stable.

"How strong are you?" Kelly asked. "Are you sitting down? Fanny got kicked, and her leg is broken."

Hanging up the kitchen phone, I raced upstairs for a phone book. Maybe a vet could still save her. My mind churned. What should I take to the barn? What would I need? When I arrived, I quickly understood that there was nothing I could do.

For once, Fanny did not whinny a welcome. Her ears were forward and alert, but her eyes were soft and her gum color pale. She was quivering even with a warm blanket that someone had put over her. She stood firmly on three legs, her left front foot dangling crookedly from a swollen crooked knee. I could see bone slivers. And it was at least two hours before a vet would be able to come and end Fanny's pain.

I remember standing in front of her with her head against my chest and her soft nose rubbing my stomach. Did she know how helpless I felt? I didn't cry. For Fanny's sake, I couldn't cry then. I left her a few times to call different vets, and I took time to call Pam and break the news. I borrowed two carrots from the neighbor who let me use her phone. Perhaps I needed those two hours to face the truth.

Kelly, Tammy, and Linda waited with me and kept us company. Fanny stood quietly with her ears forward toward me, expectantly, gobbling the hay, sometimes rubbing that upper lip against my stomach. Linda's son had taken lessons on Fanny and she brought him to say good-bye. He agreed to go in the barn when the vet arrived. Fanny had been very tolerant of his boyish awkwardness, even though her mischievous nature tested his control.

Though we had waited for hours, the vet came too soon; and I suddenly wished I could put my arms around her neck one more time. But all I could think of was to end her pain as soon as possible. Did she know what was coming? Or did she trust me to fix it? How I wished that Fanny and I could actually talk to each other! I wanted so much to tell her thank you for all she had given me. But I wouldn't have known what else to say.

For sixteen years, Fanny had been a special part of my life. I touched her neck, wanting to feel once more that place of belonging. It was there no more. Back in the barn, I passed her empty stall. The tears had waited long enough. I leaned against the post and felt Linda's arm on my shoulder. I couldn't hold back any longer.

Fanny died at 3:45 P.M. and I was supposed to work in the real estate office from 5:00 to 7:00 that evening. I quickly cleaned Dude's stall, laid out feed, hay, and water and left. I would clean Fanny's stall later. Linda said she would put Dude in when she put her own mare in. I thanked her and ran for the truck. I cried most of the way home.

I called several other realtors to take my shift, but no one could. I changed clothes, washed my face with cold water and headed for the office. The phone started ringing the moment I got there and I was busy taking messages and phone calls for the next two hours. I didn't have time to grieve.

Returning home, I called Pam. She offered the possibility of burying Fanny on her farm, about eighty miles away. Another friend had called and offered to move Fanny in their big truck and trailer, but I knew the cost of gas for that rig and I didn't want to impose on them. Pam said we would both feel better if we knew where Fanny was buried. Talking became difficult and I told Pam I'd call her back. I liked the idea of taking Fanny to Pam's farm, but I didn't know how to get her there.

I didn't mention to Pam that I had already called the rendering company. A woman had said to put her where the truck could get to her and to put a can by her head with twenty dollars in it for the driver. I called the company back and cancelled.

The first problem was Fanny's location out in the pasture, in the soft mud. The vet had suggested I try to walk her closer to the road before giving her the shot, but I refused to ask any more of her. Overnight, God solved that problem for me. By Tuesday morning, the ground was frozen.

Kelly suggested I stay away from the barn that afternoon. They moved Fanny's body closer to the road for me, only because the ground was now frozen hard enough for the tractor to handle it. Wednesday morning, as I went to the barn to clean Dude's stall, I passed a large mound by the gate covered with a pink tarp. It was still freezing cold, and I had real estate appointments and meetings all day, with no time to tend to arrangements. In the meantime, Fanny's horseshoes were removed for a keepsake, in a cold drizzling rain by Red Clark, an understanding friend.

The sun came out Thursday morning with increasing warmth. I rented a flatbed trailer with a winch and two men from the barn had offered to help. As I cleaned Fanny's stall for the last time, they put her on the flatbed and covered her with a tarp. I was adding fresh water in Dude's stall, when I heard a whinny outside that sounded just like Fanny's! The men were coming back into the barn just then, and I asked them if there was a horse outside. I told them I heard a whinny. They looked at me sympathetically and assured me there were no horses out there. *But I had heard a whinny!* It seemed to come from outside and it sounded just like Fanny! I've always wondered about that.

The men opened the gate and I drove off with my "horsey hearse," as Kelly named it. It was a beautiful day for a special journey. I had a two-hour drive to meditate on how God had worked out the details. Monday, the temperature had been in the 40s. The next two days, when I was busy with meetings, freezing temperatures had provided a way to move Fanny's body to the gate and preserved Fanny's dignity until Thursday, when I had time to take care of things.

I arrived at Pam's at noon and we took time to eat. I planned to stay overnight and return home Friday afternoon. Her farm was outside of town a few miles, and Pam rode with me to show the way. Bob was already there. Many years ago, Bob had helped Pam with Fanny's care. Pam's son, Will, came later.

Although our task was less than joyous, the afternoon was pleasant and sunny, and many details just fell in place. Bob backed the trailer over the ditch without incident to get it off the road. Not one car went by while he was blocking the road, though several passed by at other times. A tree was at the precise spot it needed to be for a pulley and rope to pull Fanny to her resting place. Later that afternoon, we witnessed the most beautiful sunset.

Fanny was buried not far from the road. On the fence nearby, I hung the horseshoe from Fanny's broken leg. Pam started a fire on the frozen ground and we all scrounged for firewood from dead trees nearby. Pam watched the fire, shifting it slightly as it softened the frozen ground. Will and Bob did most of the digging, though Pam and I did a little of it to give them a short rest.

We were still working at 9 P.M., with only the light of the fire. When the depth of the hole made visibility difficult, I gathered handfuls of dried goldenrod from the pasture, using them like a torch above the opening. Pam had brought two bales of straw, to spread under and over Fanny before covering the hole. As the men replaced the dirt, Pam and I sat on a log by the fire, talking and sipping hot soup.

Many years later, Pam and I still share a special friendship. I recently told Pam about a riding lesson on my latest horse. "She asked me to trot with my feet out of the stirrups and then to put my feet back into the stirrups while I kept trotting. You know, I hadn't realized how tense I am while riding!"

"You were always tense." Pam replied. "Remember the horse show when Fanny ran away with you? That was your own fault. She was in heat, and another horse stuck his nose where it didn't belong. Fanny tensed up and put her ears back and you got nervous and squeezed so hard that she almost jumped out from under you. But you caused it!"

The memory of that horse show, illuminated by the realization of truth, swept through my mind. As the true picture emerged, I burst out laughing.

"And you tell me now, after all these years," I retorted.

"You didn't know any better then," Pam answered softly. "You were always tense."

I remembered the day I rode Dude with Charlotte and she told me about the Sally Swift basics. That day I had seen the effects of my tenseness on Dude. When I made the effort to breathe, look up, relax in the saddle, and balance properly, Dude stopped prancing and lowered his head . . . just that quickly!

Through the years, several different instructors have told me to relax. I have a calmer horse now. Perhaps I've finally calmed down myself enough to "listen" to the instructor's directions and focus on what is happening.

Perhaps focus is the key to both learning and living . . . concentration on the moment at hand, avoiding unrelated distractions. How can I learn from a riding lesson if I'm worrying about falling off my horse! How can I enjoy life if I'm worried about all the things that could happen (and probably won't!)? But I also know that it's important to focus on God's eternal purpose above our own immediate physical desires.

One can learn so much about life from riding a horse! I've had many horses since Fanny and I've learned something valuable from every one of them. Fanny was my precious beginning toward insight on relationships, control issues, and mutual submission. *She gave me her attention, loyalty, and companionship. She gave me her life and being.* She rode the competitive trails with me and for me and she willingly gave it her all. We had a real partnership. She tried to do whatever I asked of her, even when she was frustrated with my training efforts. Even when she was hurting.

And that last morning, when she was turned out to pasture, was her ornery nature intensified by the lack of something to ease the pain? I had run out of Bute. Short on cash, I put off getting more. She had been without Bute for several days. Did I hasten the end with that one omission? Would that half-a-tablet-a-day have given her a few more years? Or was it simply that I allowed her to be turned out with another mare that had already kicked her a few months previously? I guess I could blame myself forever, or I could simply accept what happened as part of the story.

When Pam and I sat on the log that cold January night, watching the two men dig and fill the hole, we shared memories of a special horse. Pam had affectionately called Fanny the "Mahogany mare." I recalled how her fetlock hair had always grown extra long in winter, streaked with a light, golden brown. Pam called it her feathers and observers asked if she was part draft horse. I trimmed it off with scissors each spring before using clippers on her legs. I remembered how she kicked her stall much of the time, except for two weeks after I sneaked into the barn one night in the dark and gave her a good spanking! I remembered the way she always whinnied a greeting to me. And the way she rubbed her nose against my stomach before the vet came.

As always, as Pam and I talked, she shared her insight as well as her vast store of information.

"She loved you," Pam reminded me. "She tried to do everything you asked, even when she couldn't." *A deep sense of thankfulness overwhelmed me, as I thought of the joy Fanny had given me.* I remembered Job's quote, "The Lord gave, and the Lord has taken away." But what He gave would never be forgotten. It wasn't just the sixteen years of adventure with Fanny. It was years of emotional and spiritual growth resulting from the experiences of training. It was also a personal glimpse of God's eternal struggle with mankind and a vision of the glory that is possible from understanding the significance of submission (or lack thereof!).

Gazing over at the men, still shoveling frozen dirt into a dark hole on a freezing January night, Pam asked simply, "You know what this is, don't you?"

She paused a moment, watching the two men at work, giving me time to think. Then she answered her own question with a single word.

"Love."

This is how God showed His love among us: He sent His one and only Son into the world that we might live through Him. This is love: not that we loved God, but that He loved us and sent His Son as an atoning sacrifice for our sins. 1 John 4:9–10

By Sally's Permission

I first heard of Sally Swift while riding with a new friend. After seeing how her basic principles of "Centered Riding" were so effective, I audited one clinic then later participated in another.

I am honored by her written response after she read an early version of chapter 13 of this book back in 1984.

> I think you have done a remarkably good job of saying what you think and of explaining what I teach. I feel that you have given a good feel of what I try to teach and your applications are well expressed. One friend I showed it to said, "I couldn't have explained what you teach nearly as clearly as that in writing." And she has ridden with me a lot.

I am also thankful to Miss Swift for taking the time to read the entire manuscript in 1994, and I proudly share a few paragraphs of her letter back to me.

> . . . an interesting and convincing account of how the experience of working with horses and the principles of Centered Riding (emphasis on the basics) apply to the rest of life and to the spiritual dimension.

> Thank you for asking for permission to quote me fairly extensively which I am happy to grant you. May you succeed in publishing your manuscript. The turkey story is wonderful!

Sally Swift has authored two books: *Centered Riding* and *Centered Riding 2,* published in 1985 and 2002 respectively by Trafalgar Square Publishing. She also has two videos on the same material.

Thank you, Sally . . . for sharing your insightful teachings.

Betsy's Photo Album

I was almost three years old when Dad took this snap-
shot of me in the driver's seat of the corn plow with Jim
and Jack, Grandpa's team of mules.

My first real ride on a horse . . . I was eight years old! Babe was a spotted Shetland pony mare that belonged to Uncle Kent, Grandpa's brother. Uncle Kent and Aunt Lottie lived in a log cabin a few miles from Roundup, Montana.

To store hay in our barn, Bell was hitched by a "singletree" to a pulley system along the top of the barn. I led her back and forth as a large hay fork lifted chunks of loose hay out of the wagon up to a track at the top of the barn from where it was dropped into the "haymow."

In May of 1950 (I was ten years old), Grandpa lifted me up on Bell after a day's work in the field and I rode her to the water tank. After that, I rode her every chance I had!

I rode Bell even when our Iowa farm ground was covered with winter snow! Here, she wears her harness bridle with blinders.

Big 1600 pound Bell was the only "riding" horse I had until Fanny came along many years later.

Fanny as an eight-year-old. This was one of the photos I used for her Appaloosa registration papers.

I will always remember how Fanny ducked her head one day to avoid the bit, obviously playing a game with Autumn Hawkins and probably enjoying her happy giggles as much as I did!

Nicholas Campbell took a riding lesson on Fanny just a few months before her final injury. He came to tell Fanny goodbye before the vet arrived.

When she was older, Fanny was a safe mount for little girls like my young niece.

When she was seven years old, Renee Price wanted to be a jockey. She was a good riding student and Gambler was an excellent lesson pony.

Diana Nussbaum (now Diana Davolt) was more than a riding student. She was good with horses, and I was happy for her to ride Dude in a few area horse shows. She also rode Syn-cere.

When Syn-cere was nineteen years old, we entered her first Competitive Trail Ride. On her second ride that same year, we won a Fifth Place ribbon (and it was on my birthday)!

A precious keepsake is this photo of my grandfather's blacksmith shop in Center Junction, Iowa. Grandpa (Lyman E. Moats) is in the center, one arm across his waist.

The author welcomes correspondence:

Betsy Kelleher
104 Holiday Mobile Home Park
Granite City, Illinois 62040-6502

Or send e-mail: *Goduseshorses@aol.com*
Visit web site at www.Goduseshorses.com

To order additional copies of

Sometimes
a Woman Needs
a Horse

Have your credit card ready and call:

1-877-421-READ (7323)

or please visit our web site at
www.pleasantword.com

Also available at:
www.amazon.com
and
www.barnesandnoble.com

Printed in the United States
132009LV00001B/21/A